THE

GEEKS OF WAR

THE SECRETIVE LABS

AND BRILLIANT MINDS

BEHIND TOMORROW'S

WARFARE TECHNOLOGIES

JOHN EDWARDS

AMACOM

American Management Association

New York • Atlanta • Brussels • Chicago • Mexico City • San Francisco •
Shanghai • Tokyo • Toronto • Washington, D.C.

Special discounts on bulk quantities of AMACOM books are available to corporations, professional associations, and other organizations. For details, contact Special Sales Department, AMACOM, a division of American Management Association, 1601 Broadway, New York, NY 10019. Tel.: 212-903-8316. Fax: 212-903-8083. Web site: www.amacombooks.org

This publication is designed to provide accurate and authoritative information in regard to the subject matter covered. It is sold with the understanding that the publisher is not engaged in rendering legal, accounting, or other professional service. If legal advice or other expert assistance is required, the services of a competent professional person should be sought.

Library of Congress Cataloging-in-Publication Data

Edwards, John, 1954–
   The geeks of war : the secretive labs and brilliant minds behind tomorrow's warfare technologies / John Edwards.
       p.   cm.
   Includes index.
   ISBN 0-8144-0852-4
     1. Military research—United States.   2. Military art and science—Technological innovations—United States—History—21st century. I. Title.

U393.E38   2005
355'.07'0973—dc22
                                                                        2005002636

Printing number

10 9 8 7 6 5 4 3 2 1

To my parents, and the countless others,
whose wartime sacrifices paved the way
for the comfortable and free life I enjoy today.

War is an ugly thing, but not the ugliest of things: the decayed and degraded state of moral and patriotic feeling which thinks nothing *worth* a war is worse. When a people are used as mere human instruments for firing cannon or thrusting bayonets, in the service and for the selfish purposes of a master, such war degrades a people. A war to protect other human beings against tyrannical injustice; a war to give victory to their own ideas of right and good, and which is their own war, carried on for an honest purpose by their free choice, is often the means of their regeneration. A man who has nothing which he is willing to fight for, nothing which he cares more about than he does about his personal safety, is a miserable creature who has no chance of being free, unless made and kept so by the exertions of better men than himself. As long as justice and injustice have not terminated *their* ever-renewing fight for ascendancy in the affairs of mankind, human beings must be willing, when need is, to do battle for the one against the other.

—John Stuart Mill (1806–1873), "The Contest in America," *Dissertations and Discussions,* vol. 1, p. 26 (1868). First published in *Fraser's Magazine,* February 1862.

[CONTENTS]

I like to think that some good can come out of almost anything. My background is essential to this belief. That's because I'm a product of World War II, and while I like to believe that I'm a good man, it's hard to think of anything worse than total warfare.

DAD

My father, John George Edwards, was a British soldier, part of the historic force that drove across northern Europe in the weeks after D-Day. In my father's case, the word *drove* is particularly apt. That's because his job was to drive generals and other top military leaders to wherever they needed to go—often to dangerous places on the front lines of battle. My father literally drove the officers (and himself) through France, Belgium, Holland, and into Germany.

At the end of his journey, my father arrived in Hamburg. By the war's end, the great port city had been transformed into a titanic pile of rubble, thanks to the unceasing efforts of Air Chief Marshal Sir Arthur Harris, Bomber Command, and the U.S. Army Air Forces. Attached to army's occupation headquarters, my father continued to drive the brass to various locations in and around the city (not an easy job, considering the devastation of the local infrastructure).

One night, on a blind date set up by one of his mates, my father met a local woman who, some 9 years later, would become my mother.

FIGURE A–1.   DAD.

MAM

To say that by 1945 Gerda Auguste Elisabeth Menzer Metzner had lived a difficult 22 years would be to commit a serious, almost ridiculous understatement. While my father had experienced what might be called a humble life (he was the son of a Royal Navy stoker, and the family never had much money), my mother's life was particularly ugly.

FIGURE A—2. MAM.

Mam was just 6 months younger than my father, but had already lived a life that would have stretched the imagination of the most florid soap opera writer. By the time she met Dad, she had survived one of history's worst economic collapses, not to mention 6 years of war and the death of her first husband, Martin Metzner, a naval officer, who was killed in action off the coast of Crete.[1] For my mother, a lasting reminder of Martin's love was their daughter, Christine, born less than 3 weeks after his death (during an air raid).

My mother, like almost everyone else in Hamburg, was desperately, agonizingly, almost unimaginably poor.[2] The war had killed over 3.5 million German fighting men, so it appeared likely that my mother would remain a widow, and probably poor, for the rest of her life. A probable scenario . . . at least until she met Dad.

My parents' courtship was fast, but not entirely smooth. After all, my father spoke no German and my mother, and her family, spoke no English. Still, I'm sure that Dad made quite an impression on my mother's family. For instance, the first time he was invited to my grandparents' apartment, he brought along his rifle. Well, it *was* enemy territory.

TOGETHER

Just a few months after my parents met, Dad received the news that he would soon be sent back to England and mustered out of the army. By that time, however, my parents knew that they wanted to be together for life (as they were, until Dad's death in 1978). My mother spent the next few months making plans to move to England, which she did in 1947, my sister in tow. They were married shortly thereafter. Mam didn't exactly receive a warm welcome in my father's hometown, Portsmouth. The local population, quite understandably, was still feeling belligerent toward Germany and Germans. My mother didn't help things much by speaking to my sister in German both inside and outside the home. She had no choice, really, since neither could yet speak English.

FIGURE A—3.   WEDDING DAY.

England may have won the war, but most people didn't feel like celebrating. Jobs were scarce and most of life's essentials, even clothes and furniture, were still rationed. Mam could have lived with that; things were hardly better back in Germany. What she couldn't live with was Dad's mother (whose husband had died a few years earlier, not due to anything connected with the war). Supposedly, after one vigorous argument, my grandmother chased after Mam with a kitchen knife. I have no idea whether this really happened, or if Grams really intended to kill my mother, but I do know that Mam wanted to move out of Grams's house as soon as possible. The problem was that homes were as scarce as everything else—perhaps even more so—and it appeared that my parents would have to continue living with Grams for the foreseeable future. That situation might very well have led to renewed total warfare between the Germans and English (at least on a one-to-one level).

Fortunately, Mam had an out. Before the war, a cousin and her husband had moved from Germany to America. They were now American citizens, successfully established in business, and willing to sponsor my parents. So after discussing the situation for a while, my parents decided to emigrate to the United States, leaving Europe and all their troubles behind. They arrived in New York on the RMS *Queen Mary* in October 1949. Life suddenly became a lot less tumultuous.

SO HERE WE ARE

Why am I telling you all of this? After all, there's not much cutting-edge technology research in my parents' saga. And, to be honest, Mam and Dad came out of the war in much better shape than many other unfortunate souls. The point I want to make is the one I mentioned at the top of this story: that some good can come out of anything.

War is often (but not always) a necessary evil. Despite all the suffering that took place, the world is a much better place today because the Allies won World War II. Technology played a big part in the war's ultimate resolution. Without the edge that inventions such as radar, electronic computers, and improved land, sea, and air vehicles gave the Allies, the war probably would have lasted many more years and might have ended with different victors.

While a good case can be made for the fact that technology intensified the suffering for everyone involved in the war, it's also true that technological progress is inevitable. To wish away new military technologies simply because they are powerful and destructive is like trying to ignore a tornado. You can't stop nature, and you can't stop progress. Since history has shown that people tend to use the weapons they have at their disposal (a chilling thought in this nuclear and biotechnological age), I would prefer that the forces of freedom have the best weapons and related technologies that are available. That's what our research scientists are developing, and that's what I'm proud to describe in this book.

I think Mam and Dad would have wanted it that way.

John Edwards, Gilbert, Arizona, 2004

NOTES

1. In 1922, the year my mother was born, a loaf of bread cost 163 marks. By my mother's first birthday, the price had risen to 200,000,000,000 marks; among the many bombing raids my mother survived was the July 1943 attack that virtually destroyed the city of Hamburg. In one night alone, over 40,000 people died in a single raid that created the first man-made firestorm.
2. By April 1945, *weekly* food rations, per adult, were 900 grams of bread (1.9 pounds), 137 grams of meat (4.8 ounces), and 75 grams of fats (1.7 pounds).

THE MILITARY–
TECHNOLOGY MATRIX

WHAT DO THE AEGIS WEAPONS SYSTEM, B-2 Spirit, and Tomahawk cruise missiles have in common? Well, they are all amazing technologies that were once simply good ideas. Technology moves from "good idea" to an actual, battle-ready technology by following a long, complex, and often circuitous route.

Many new technologies, for example, bunker-busting bombs, rise out of a need created by a national policy, such as overthrowing Saddam Hussein in Iraq. Others are developed simply because a technology becomes available to accomplish a specific task (an artificial intelligence breakthrough that allows aircraft to fly themselves is a good example). The actual process by which technologies are adopted by the military is one that relies on complex interrelations between individuals and groups within the government's executive and legislative branches, as well as input from the media and public.

TECHNOLOGY AND THE
EXECUTIVE BRANCH

The U.S. Government's executive branch, which includes the offices of president, vice president, departments, and independent agencies, has a major influence on military technology research, perhaps greater than in any other area of government.

The Department of Defense

The executive branch entity primarily responsible for setting and directing military technology priorities is, of course, the Department of Defense (DoD). The DoD includes many departments that study and propose emerging technologies. In fact, just about every part of the DoD is focused in one way or another on technology, since it is so crucial to the nation's war-fighting abilities.

At the top of the DoD's military technology command ladder is the Under Secretary of Defense for Acquisition, Technology, and Logistics, or the USD (AT&L). Under the authority, direction, and control of the Secretary of Defense, the USD (AT&L) is the principal staff assistant and advisor to the Secretary and Deputy Secretary of Defense for all matters relating to the DoD Acquisition System: research and development; advanced technology; developmental testing and evaluation; production; logistics; installation management; military construction; procurement; environment security; and nuclear, chemical, and biological matters.

The USD (AT&L)'s responsibilities include the establishment and publication of policies and procedures governing the operations of the DoD Acquisition System and the administrative oversight of defense contractors. Other responsibilities include the coordination of research and development programs DoD-wide to eliminate duplication of effort and ensure that available resources are used to maximum advantage. The USD (AT&L) is also charged with establishing policies and programs that:

- Strengthen DoD component technology development programs,

- Encourage technical competition and technology-driven prototyping that promise increased military capabilities, and

- Exploit the cost-reduction potential of innovative or commercially developed technologies.

Serving under the USD (AT&L) are several deputies who are responsible for specific military technologies. These include the Director of Defense Research and Engineering, the Deputy Under Secretary of Defense (Acquisition and Technology), the Deputy Under Secretary of Defense (Logistics and Material Readiness), the Assistant to the Secretary of Defense (Nuclear and Chemical and Biological Defense Programs), the Deputy Under Secretary of Defense (Advanced Systems and Concepts), and the Deputy Under Secretary of Defense (Science and Technology).

The Defense Advanced Research Projects Agency

The Defense Advanced Research Projects Agency (DARPA) is the DoD's central research and development organization. It manages and directs selected basic and applied research and development projects for the DoD, and pursues research and technology where risk and payoff are both very high and where success may provide dramatic advances for traditional military roles and missions. As shown in the upcoming chapters, DARPA has a hand in a wide array of promising technologies.

The National Science and Technology Council

Like the DoD, the White House has its own technology advisors. The National Science and Technology Council (NSTC) was established by executive order in 1993. This cabinet-level council is the principal means for the president to coordinate the science, space, and technology components of the federal research and development enterprise. The president chairs the NSTC. Other members are the vice president, assistant to the president for science and technology, cabinet secretaries and agency heads with significant science and technology responsibilities, and other White House officials. An important objective of the NSTC is the establishment of clear national goals for federal science and technology investments in areas ranging from information technologies and health research, to improving transportation systems and strengthening fundamental research. The council prepares research and development strategies that are coordinated across federal agencies to form an investment package aimed at accomplishing multiple national goals.

The President's Council of Advisors on Science and Technology

On September 30, 2001, President George W. Bush signed an executive order to form the President's Council of Advisors on Science and Technology (PCAST). PCAST was originally established by President George H.W. Bush in 1990 to enable the president to receive advice from the private sector and academic community on technology, scientific research priorities, and math and science education. The organization follows a tradition of presidential advisory panels on science and technology dating back to Presidents Eisenhower and Truman. The council members, distinguished individuals appointed by the president, are drawn from industry, education, and research institutions and other nongovernmental organizations.

The National Science Foundation

While not specifically charged with the development of defense technologies, the National Science Foundation (NSF) sponsors numerous research projects with potential military applications.

The NSF is an independent agency of the U.S. Government, established by the National Science Foundation Act of 1950. The NSF consists of the National Science Board of twenty-four part-time members and a director (who also serves as ex officio National Science Board member), each appointed by the president with the advice and consent of the U.S. Senate. Other senior officials include a deputy director, appointed by the president with the advice and consent of the U.S. Senate, and eight assistant directors.

The NSF's mission is to recommend and encourage the pursuit of national policies for the promotion of basic research and education in the sciences and engineering. The agency also works to strengthen research and education innovation in the sciences and engineering throughout the United States, including independent research by individuals.

A key part of the NSF's role in the development of military technologies is the initiation and support, through grants and contracts, of scientific and engineering research and programs. Through these deals, the NSF is looking to strengthen scientific and engineering research potential at all levels.

The National Security Agency

The National Security Agency (NSA) is the nation's cryptologic (encoding/deciphering) organization. The NSA coordinates, directs, and performs highly specialized activities to protect U.S. information systems and produce foreign intelligence information. A high-technology organization, NSA is on the frontiers of communications and data processing. The organization is currently in the process of expanding its outreach to external laboratories. The NSA's research interests include signal processing, computers, communications and networking, microelectronics, and advanced mathematics.

The Central Intelligence Agency

The CIA often farms out research and development work to government, university, and corporate laboratories.

CONGRESS AND TECHNOLOGY

Numerous congressional committees have military technology oversight. These committees compete with executive branch offices to define and set national defense technology priorities. Political influence from lobbyists representing defense companies, universities, and other interested parties also plays a major role in deciding which technologies Congress considers or rejects.

Congress also holds the purse strings that control military spending. So by deciding whether to fund or not to fund a specific project, or by simply ignoring a project, Congress can decide whether a good idea ever becomes a reality.

The Office of Science and Technology Policy

Congress established OSTP in 1976 with a broad mandate to advise the president and others in the executive branch on the impact of science and technology on domestic and international affairs. The 1976 act also authorizes OSTP to lead an interagency effort to develop and implement sound science and technology policies and budgets and to work with the private sector, state and local governments, the science and higher education communities, and other nations toward this end. OSTP also provides technical support to the Department of Homeland Security.

The National Critical Technologies List

Compiled by OSTP, this "want list" of technologies inspires laboratories to pursue specific avenues of research, often at the detriment of promising technologies that do not make the government's list.

The most recent list, released in 2004, identifies needs in the following areas:

Energy

Energy Efficiency

Energy Storage,
  Conditioning,
  Distribution, and
  Transmission

Improved Generation

Environmental Quality

Monitoring and
  Assessment

Pollution Control

Remediation and
  Restoration

Information and Communications

Components

Communications

Computer Systems

Information Management

Intelligent Complex
  Adaptive Systems

Sensors

Software and Toolkits

Living Systems

Biotechnology

Medical Technologies

Agriculture and Food
Technologies

Human Systems

Manufacturing

Discrete Product
Manufacturing

Continuous Process
Manufacturing

Micro/Nano Fabrication
and Machining

Materials

Materials

Structures

Transportation

Aerodynamics

Avionics and Controls

Propulsion and Power

Systems Integration

Human Interface

TECHNOLOGY AND THE MEDIA

By presenting news and viewpoints, the media plays a crucial role in molding public opinion on various potential military technologies.

Television

By showcasing advanced technologies operating in both simulated and real-world conditions, TV can shift public opinion toward or away from developing technologies.

Print and Web Media

Like their partners in television, newspapers and magazines, in print and online, influence defense military technology policy by promoting and discouraging the development of specific technologies.

Technology Trade Press

Although largely unrecognized by the general public, the technology trade press influences defense technology choices by permitting research labs to fight public relations battles on their pages.

THE LABYRINTH

As we've just seen, the national military–technology infrastructure is a labyrinth. It works with—and occasionally against—military, civilian, government, academic, and corporate laboratories. Fights between the various departments, offices, and councils are not uncommon, and sometimes they appear to work at cross-purposes. As with most everything in Washington, politics and money lie at the heart of most military technology decisions. Often, the research lab with the strongest backing by a corporation or an influential local congressional representative receives the funds to pursue a new technology.

Wars are fought on the battlefield, but the technologies that enable twenty-first-century warfare are often funded by government, and developed inside research laboratories. Within the walls of academic and government labs, highly skilled researchers (self-professed geeks, for the most part) are probing the edges of science to uncover technologies that promise to make warfare both more efficient and deadly. The following chapters show how this cumbersome military–technology matrix strives to foster new technologies that promise to augment and support the nation's military.

The Geeks of War provides an in-depth look at the research that is rapidly and relentlessly creating the next generation of military technologies. In writing this book, I have examined scores of advanced technologies, including tactical, information, communication, vehicular, biological, and cryptographic systems, as well as their multiple and often complex scientific, political, and economic implications.

As you read, it is important to remember that this is not a compendium of all emerging military technologies. Information on many budding technologies is classified or exists only in a researcher's mind, making it impossible to write about them. In addition, many new technologies that have debuted over the past several years or that are so far along in their development that they are already well embedded in the public consciousness have not been included. In other words, if you want to read about the F-35 Joint Strike Fighter or V-22 Osprey, you'll have to look elsewhere.

I like to think of this book as something of an adventure, a journey inside leading military technology research facilities, a clandestine world that very few ordinary people ever see. Academic labs profiled in *The Geeks of War* include such notable bodies as the Massachusetts Institute of Technology, the Georgia Institute of Technology, Carnegie Mellon University, Harvard University, Penn State University, Johns Hopkins University, and Northwestern University. Government labs covered by this book include the Office of Naval Research, the U.S. Army Soldier Systems Center, the National Institute of Standards and Technology, the U.S. Space and Missile Defense Command, and the Oak Ridge National Laboratory.

Gee whiz is a silly and corny expression, but I have to admit there is an awful lot of gee whiz in *The Geeks of War*. After all, it's hard to describe things like robots and death rays without having at least a little bit of a gee-whiz attitude. So, gee whiz it is. The geeks themselves (and the author, too) wouldn't want it any other way.

In the end, my goal in writing this book has been to peer inside academic and government research laboratories to find out what may become real-world military technologies within 5 or 10 years. I've aimed to provide as much cutting-edge information as possible, to survey technologies that aren't generally known yet, and to offer an overview of where military research technology is headed.

I'll leave it up to you to judge whether I've succeeded in my mission.

CHAPTER ONE

FINDING AND BREAKING THINGS

TACTICAL SYSTEMS

THE MAIN POINT OF WAR, of course, is to find and break things. If you find enough of the enemy's things and break them, and then show the capacity to keep on breaking things—especially if you do it with precision—the enemy loses its ability to wage war and gives up. It's that simple, really. Kindergarten stuff on a horrific level.

Tactical weapons are the devices armies use to break things. The oldest tactical weapon is the rock. Cheap and readily available in most places, rocks were the preferred weapon for untold millennia. Rocks can be thrown by hand, dropped from structures (like castle walls), or, with the help of inventions such as slingshots and catapults, propelled over long distances.

Over the past several thousand years, rocks were gradually replaced by an array of new weapons, including arrows, bullets, grenades (a kind of explosive rock), and hydrogen bombs (really powerful explosive rocks). Delivery system technology has also moved forward: Human arms, slingshots, and catapults have been replaced by guns, cannons, rockets, airplanes, and dozens of other systems.

When will it all end? Probably never. Unless we annihilate our-selves (unlikely) or find a way to live in universal peace (even more unlikely), people will keep looking for better, faster, cheaper, and easier ways to break things. It's called progress.

THE OBJECTIVE FORCE WARRIOR: HIGH-TECH SOLDIER

Arnold Schwarzenegger as the Terminator has nothing over the Objective Force Warrior (OFW). The army's goal is to develop a high-tech soldier with 20 times the capability of today's warrior and to have that soldier commissioned by about 2010. With advanced technologies, the army plans to create an overmatch and greatly minimize the danger to its soldiers.

"With the Objective Force Warrior, the army wants to stretch the bounds of technology but still have something that is feasible and can be built," says George Fisher of the Oak Ridge National Laboratory's (ORNL) National Security Directorate. The ORNL is collaborating with the army on the project. "The army wants an independent look into the future to see what emerging technologies and innovative combinations of these concepts might allow." Because of ORNL's unique capabilities and its connections to indus-try, colleges, and universities, the army has asked the laboratory to coordinate a unique "visioning" process. "What we're calling 'the art of the possible' in enabling technologies will leverage the Depart-ment of Energy's considerable investment and technologies," Fisher says. Concept design panels have been established, composed of futurists, systems engineers, biologists, military experts, human fac-tors specialists, writers, and others of diverse backgrounds.

The goal is to develop innovative technologies that allow a soldier to engage and destroy the enemy at longer ranges with greater precision and with devastating results, according to Fisher. Technologies to make this possible include:

- Better communications devices.
- Advanced situational awareness software, such as a highly accurate global positioning system (GPS).

- Chemical-biological (chembio) detection and protection systems.

- Advanced weapons and protective equipment. Fatigues and flak jackets of the past, for example, would be replaced by a system designed to better protect a soldier and provide hemorrhage control in case a bullet penetrates. The helmet of the future warrior might be a sealed unit that contains communications, vision enhancements, a laser for target ranging and a heads-up display.

To provide a glimpse into the future, one of the panels submitted a hypothetical letter from a soldier to his parents dated October 30, 2017. In the letter, the young soldier writes:

My suit has the ability to stop a rifle bullet. It is made of a material that is as flexible as my football jersey but gets hard as steel when a bullet or knife is pushed into it. The material has some kind of chemical in it that lets fresh air pass through it but stops and destroys chemical warfare agents. If I do get injured, the suit automatically inflates over the wound, stopping the bleeding and applying medicine to the injury until our medic can come help me.

The letter continues:

Remember how you used to tell me that playing all those video games wouldn't get me anywhere in life? You have to see my helmet to believe it. It's like an IMAX movie right before my eyes.

The helmet of the future will allow a soldier to monitor power reserves, show the range of an enemy, and provide an enormous amount of additional information, including the enemy's capabilities (for example, data on the types and sizes of weapons at their disposal). While many of the technologies to make the Objective Force Warrior a reality are maturing today, several others, called breakthrough technologies, have yet to be developed. These include advanced fuel cells, exoskeletons, directed-energy lethal and nonlethal weapons, and lethal robotics. The exoskeleton would augment the strength of a soldier and enhance mobility, speed, endurance, range, and load-carrying capabilities.

STAR WARS PLUS: BATTLE LASERS

Laser weapons? The concept may not be as exotic as fans of Luke Skywalker once thought, thanks to recent leaps forward in the development of a powerful free-electron laser (FEL), which provides intense, powerful beams of laser light that can be tuned to a precise color or wavelength. In fact, FELs have been shown to generate very large amounts of power, tunable from the microwave to the visible spectrum. They do so by absorbing and releasing energy at any wavelength, which is possible as the electrons are freed of atoms, and it is this key feature that enables the FEL to be controlled more precisely than conventional lasers to produce intense, powerful light in brief bursts with extreme precision.

The Office of Naval Research (ONR) is interested in developing FEL technology that is an electrically driven, tunable laser operated at infrared wavelengths (where light is most efficiently transmitted in the atmosphere) for potential applications in shipboard defense. "What does that mean?" asks Gil Graff, an ONR project manager. "Think USS *Cole*. Think what might have been done to prevent such an attack." Think about it: The immediate threat to any surface combatant is the anti-ship cruise missile with its stealthy, sea-skimming characteristics that reduce the time any defensive weapon system has to react. FELs could meet that threat using its speed-of-light engagement, high hit probability, and unlimited firing capability. Its low utilization cost is an added benefit.

The research is being performed at the Department of Energy's Thomas Jefferson National Accelerator Facility in Newport News, Virginia. Research paid off in mid-June 2004 when Jefferson scientists produced "first light" with a new 10-kilowatt FEL system. ONR and the Jefferson team hope to use the FEL to generate 10 kilowatts of infrared light and 1 kilowatt of ultraviolet light. That's not quite enough power to blow things out of the skies as in the movies, but it is a big step toward building an important new tactical weapon.

As Graff puts it, "The original 1-kilowatt FEL exceeded the

navy's goals and expectations; no less is expected from the upgraded FEL. This is exciting."

WEAPONS REVOLUTION: THE FORCE OF GAMMA RAYS

An exotic kind of nuclear explosive being developed by the DoD could blur the critical distinction between conventional and nuclear weapons. The work has also raised fears that weapons based on this technology could trigger the next arms race.

New Scientist reported in August 2003 that the explosive works by stimulating the release of energy from the nuclei of certain elements without nuclear fission or fusion. The energy, emitted as gamma radiation, is thousands of times greater than that from conventional chemical explosives. The technology has already been included in the DoD's Militarily Critical Technologies List, which states: "Such extraordinary energy density has the potential to revolutionize all aspects of warfare."

Scientists have known for many years that the nuclei of some elements, such as hafnium, can exist in a high-energy state, or nuclear isomer, that slowly decays to a low-energy state by emitting gamma rays. For example, hafnium178m2, the excited, isomeric form of hafnium-178, has a half-life of 31 years. The possibility that this process could be explosive was discovered when Carl Collins and colleagues at the University of Texas—Dallas demonstrated that they could artificially trigger the decay of the hafnium isomer by bombarding it with low-energy X-rays. The experiment released 60 times as much energy as was put in, and, in theory, a much greater energy release could be achieved.

The effect of a nuclear-isomer explosion would be to release high-energy gamma rays capable of killing any living thing in the immediate area, according to the *New Scientist*. It would cause little fallout compared to a fission explosion, but any undetonated isomer would be dispersed as small radioactive particles, making it a somewhat "dirty" bomb. This material could cause long-term health problems for anybody who breathed it.

The DoD notes that there are serious technical issues to be overcome and that useful applications may be decades away. But its Militarily Critical Technologies List also notes: "We should remember that less than 6 years intervened between the first scientific publication characterizing the phenomenon of fission and the first use of a nuclear weapon in 1945."

BETTER WARHEADS THROUGH PLASTICS

Shooting down enemy air threats—whether ballistic missiles, cruise missiles, or aircraft—is a tactical problem that leaves little room for error. The targets move fast and must be verifiably, catastrophically, destroyed. An incoming missile hit and broken into pieces by an air defense missile can be as dangerous as one that lands intact. The Iraqi Scud missile that killed so many American troops at their Saudi base during the 1991 Gulf War is sad evidence of that risk—it had apparently been hit by a Patriot missile on its way down, but its warhead functioned on impact nonetheless. So the navy's goal in improving the effectiveness of its air defense warheads is to enable them to inflict enough damage on an incoming missile to destroy it at a safe distance.

The Office of Naval Research is working toward this goal. ONR's Reactive Materials Enhanced Warhead Program seeks to demonstrate missile warheads that achieve visible catastrophic structural defeat of cruise missiles and manned aircraft. These new warheads enhance the kinetic energy of inert fragments with chemical energy released when reactive fragments hit the target. (Kinetic energy is simply the energy a body has by virtue of its motion. For example, a linebacker brings down a running back through application of his kinetic energy; a thrown rock breaks a window by transferring its kinetic energy to the glass. Chemical energy is released in the form of heat and pressure, as when, for example, something burns rapidly. A gas main explosion or the detonation of a stick of dynamite are good examples of the release of chemical energy.) The Reactive Materials Warhead combines both effects to increase the odds of destroying the target.

The new warhead uses a carefully designed chemical reaction to release heat and overpressure. These add to the destructive effect of the warhead fragments' kinetic energy as they strike the target. The fragments are composed of an advanced composite material made of powdered metal embedded in a plastic matrix that survives the explosive launch typical of warhead fragmentation. It promises potential lethality improvements of up to 500 percent.

This new reactive composite material was recently incorporated into a prototype warhead and used in a live-fire explosive static arena test against real and threat-representative targets. The demonstration showed that the new type of warhead has twice the lethal radius of its predecessors and improved structural target damage. The test results and engineering tool sets developed from this program are now being used to prepare the Reactive Material Enhanced Warhead for transition into navy missile programs that include the STANDARD Missile, the High-Speed Anti-Radiation Missile (HARM), the Advanced Medium Range Air-to-Air Missile (AMRAAM), the Sidewinder, and the Rolling Airframe Missile (RAM).

CERAMIC ARMOR: STOPS BULLETS COLD

Military helicopters, combat vehicles, and even limousines can be made safer with an improved armor developed by researchers at the DoD's Oak Ridge National Laboratory. Tests at the lab show that tiles made of ORNL's boron carbide ceramic and facings made of polymer matrix composites provide superior ability to stop armor-piercing bullets than commercially available ceramic armor.

Compared to steel, the ceramic material is 2 to 3 times harder and less than half the weight, yet it features greater stopping power. In tests performed at a ballistics range, the ceramic tiles sandwiched by four layers of a polymer matrix composite stopped 30-caliber armor-piercing bullets traveling up to 2,800 feet per second. "The hardness of the ceramic fractures the bullet, making it easier to stop small fragments," according to Steve Nunn of the lab's metals and ceramics division. Nunn and colleagues plan to conduct tests to shed more light on why ORNL's tile provides up to 24 percent better performance than commercially available ceramic tiles and why ORNL's composite facing improves the ballistic performance of a commercial armor tile by 40 percent.

SECRETS OF THE DEEP: BREAKTHROUGH MINE DETECTION

Since 1776, when naval mines were invented, navies have rightfully feared these stealthy and relatively simple weapons, which can disable or destroy warships and paralyze vital shipping. Navies worldwide employ a host of mine-detection technologies and techniques, most of them complicated, expensive, and far from perfect. So a simpler, more effective method for detecting these mines, developed by a physicist at North Carolina State University, could make big waves in naval headquarters around the globe.

Unlike current mine-detection methods, this patented technique finds objects buried in the ocean floor. Instead of complex, unreliable modeling and without the usual array of sonar transmitters and receivers, the return echo of a sonar transceiver's "ping" is recorded; it then time-reverses and the signal is transmitted. The echo that follows clearly shows buried objects, and suppresses the response from the seafloor itself, making the underwater terrain "transparent."

In 2003, David M. Pierson, a doctoral student in physics at North Carolina State, demonstrated the new approach in research he conducted with David E. Aspnes, Distinguished Professor of Physics. The project was supported by a grant from the Office of Naval Research. Pierson has since joined the Applied Physics Laboratory of Johns Hopkins University in Baltimore, where his work is supported in part by the U.S. Navy. "The method has not been explored as a solution to this problem until now," says Pierson. "Using time reversal on the return echoes back-scattered by buried mines gave us results we considered amazing."

According to Aspnes, the young physicist's research is a breakthrough. "Time reversal is a technique that has been used before in various contexts, including optics and acoustics, but before Pierson's work the advantages of time reversal for isolating targets in back-scattered signals was never before recognized."

According to Pierson, using time reversal to find buried mines requires only one transceiver, although more can be used, and the method isn't limited by the composition of the ocean floor. "Previous methods had to incorporate a lot of complex modeling of the seafloor and the ocean environment," Pierson says, "and required sophisticated software and hardware systems. My time-reversal technique not only simplifies the needed equipment, but also can be implemented using existing sonar equipment, with minor software changes. More elaborate analyses of echoes are also made possible."

What Pierson has done, says Aspnes, is to demonstrate a new approach that uses sonar but is simpler and works better than any previous method. "In Pierson's approach," he says, "a 'ping' is first transmitted from a sonar transceiver. The return echo is then recorded, time-reversed, and transmitted. He discovered that in the next echo the response from the seafloor was suppressed, but the echo from buried objects was enhanced. This enhancement is seen even if the signal from the buried object is too small to be detected in the first return."

The NC State discovery should please naval mine-detection experts, who now use everything from dolphins to divers to sophisticated software modeling and elaborate sonar arrays in their grim work, and it should send those who design such mines back to their equally grim drawing boards.

AN EXPLOSION THAT IS NOT AN EXPLOSION: BOMB BLAST SIMULATOR

Just as important as developing increasingly powerful and more stealthy tactical systems is the need to protect people and property against various types of weapons. Unfortunately, defense-focused research has suffered in recent years, with funds flowing increasingly toward offensive technologies. The fact is, according to many military planners and researchers, defensive tools have had a bad "aura." They bring to mind images of fallout shelters and other failed technologies of the past, such as France's notorious Maginot Line. Now, due to the sudden and urgent need to protect both soldiers and civilians against sudden attack, defensive systems have rapidly returned to the spotlight.

To help bolster the defensive systems research, structural engineers at the University of California—San Diego's Jacobs School of Engineering will test the effects of bomb blasts in a new blast simulator laboratory under construction at UCSD. The facility will be the world's first designed to study structural damage caused by bomb blasts without creating actual explosions. The researchers will also test new technologies to harden buildings against bomb blasts, including a UCSD composite overlay technique (originally designed to protect structures from earthquakes), which has proven effective in full-scale explosive blast tests and has been deployed abroad in several U.S. buildings.

The Explosive Loading Laboratory Testing Program is supported through a $4.2 million contract from the Technical Support Working Group (TSWG), a federal interagency organization for combating terrorism. TSWG has named UCSD as one of its primary contractors in the focus area of blast mitigation. A key deliverable in the program will be a design manual describing proven methods for hardening high-risk buildings against terrorist bomb blasts.

"Today, designing buildings that are blast resistant is more of an art than a science," says Frieder Seible, dean of the Jacobs School and principal investigator on the project. "The controlled and repeatable tests we will do with the blast simulator will allow us to create and validate computer tools that can then be used to tailor the design and assessment of important facilities." Currently, such tests are primarily designed on computers, using best-guess calculations, rather than in real-world environments.

Bomb blasts damage buildings by creating shock waves—

moving air with such force and velocity that the pulses literally push and pull structural walls and columns. When key load-bearing components begin to fail, it can lead to the progressive collapse of the entire building. The UCSD blast simulator will recreate the speed and force of explosive shock waves through servo-controlled hydraulic actuators (powerful automatic rams). Researchers will perform blast simulations on critical load-bearing elements (for example, columns, beams and girders, walls, and floors), and on nonstructural elements such as curtain walls and windows (Fig. 1–1). The machine is being designed by Jacobs School structural engineers and MTS Systems, a company that has created other velocity-generating test laboratories for automotive crash tests and military weapons tests.

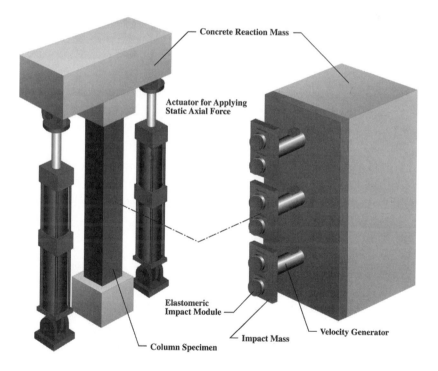

Blast Simulation Column Test

FIGURE 1–1.   BLAST SIMULATOR.

The blast simulator is an extension of the UCSD Powell Structural Research Laboratories, and is located at a new field station 8 miles east of the UCSD campus at Camp Elliott.

The new TSWG contract continues the ongoing (since 1998) UCSD research to apply earthquake retrofit techniques to harden buildings against bomb blasts. A series of full-scale explosive tests have yielded dramatic results, showing that load-bearing columns wrapped with UCSD carbon composite overlays can withstand the impact of bomb blasts with little structural damage. Since the testing began, several embassies and military installations have been retrofitted with UCSD's overlay technology. Another UCSD seismic retrofit technique—placing steel jackets around concrete columns—has also proven successful in hardening buildings against bomb blasts in the test series.

"These technologies mitigate damage to buildings by confining and containing concrete in load-bearing columns. We're actually strengthening columns so that they can take large structural deformations such as bending or swaying without collapsing," says Seible. "Also, concrete is brittle and can break apart in an explosion, but when we wrap it with these materials we can contain the concrete for the short duration of the shock wave."

Seible says the team is refining the steel jacket and carbon overlay techniques for blast mitigation through experiments in the new simulator, and addressing another challenge: how to strengthen walls and floors, as well as nonstructural elements such as curtain walls and infill walls, so that they can move during a blast without causing buildings to collapse.

SMART BOMBS: REDUCING COLLATERAL DAMAGE

The collateral damage caused by carpet bombing has compelled the U.S. military to develop more precise air-to-surface missiles. This technology is based on a combination of radar sensors, global positioning systems, and inertial navigation systems.

Improving the accuracy of munitions will not only minimize

civilian casualties and the destruction of infrastructure, but also reduce the number of weapons that need to be fired. A major British aerospace company has developed a tiny, silicon ring–based inertial measurement unit, using MEMS (microelectromechanical systems) technology, to help guide projectiles to their targets accurately. MEMs are tiny mechanical devices built into silicon chips, increasingly used to make a wide array of devices, including pressure, temperature, chemical, and vibration sensors, as well as accelerometers for air bags, pacemakers, and games. The technology is also used to make ink-jet printheads and microactuators for disk drive read/write heads.

At present, gyroscopes—ancient, clunky, low-tech devices— are used in guidance systems. "The main advantages of solid-state measurement units over conventional gyroscope-based solutions are that they have a longer life, modest manufacturing costs, and higher reliability," says Michael Valenti, an analyst with Technical Insights Aerospace and Defense Technology Research Service, located in Palo Alto, California. "The silicon technology that these systems rely on also minimizes the size, weight, and power consumption of the units."

Because some of these MEMS devices are rugged enough to withstand acceleration forces exceeding 20,000 times the force of gravity, they are being incorporated into next-generation, shoulder-launched, anti-armor rockets for use by the British and Swedish forces. The U.S. Army and Marines will incorporate these guidance systems in their helicopter rockets, while the U.S. Navy will use them to improve the accuracy of ground-support fire.

Britain's Royal Air Force and Royal Navy have been supplied with laser-guided, precision bomb systems that are not affected by bad weather or smoke. Their anti-jamming and anti-spoofing (spoofs are false direction signals sent by an enemy) technologies maintain the intended projectile of the missiles and help minimize unwanted damage.

For small combat units, situational awareness is vital. WSI Corp's InFlight system, for example, was specifically designed as an in-flight decision support aid for pilots along with the company's high-quality weather information systems. Its lightweight receiver can operate at up to 55,000 feet at temperatures ranging from −20 to +70°C.

Small, corporate aircraft have multifunction displays of important flight information including air-traffic and terrain features that give pilots time to adjust their flight plan. "Pilots and battlefield commanders have several satellite communication systems that link them to different military units," notes Valenti. "However, the U.S. Government is looking to replace several of these bulky, complex systems."

The U.S. military intends to simplify aeronautical communications by developing digital tactical systems that are compact and simple. For instance, the all-digital receiver directly digitizes incoming radio-frequency signals to provide greater support to signal processing in diverse military applications, including ground, sea, and air missions.

A promising tactical communications system is the light and small heterojunction bipolar transistor (HBT), a relatively new type of transistor that offers superior performance in microwave and millimeter-wave application. Since HBTs can transmit information twice as fast as conventional transistors, radios can be developed that will handle data much faster than conventional units. The adaptability of the digital communications devices and clarity of audio are of immense use in military operations.

SMART WEAPONS: INSECT VISION

The next generation of smart weapons may "see" targets with a man-made version of that wonder of the natural world, the insect eye. Inspired by the panoramic and precise vision of flies and other insects, researchers at several universities and institutions are working on biologically inspired "eyes" for smart weapons and other self-guided machines.

At the University of Florida, the focus of bio-optics synthetic systems research is on adapting mechanisms called photon sieves for visual purposes. "We think we can use this concept to make smart weapons smarter," says Paul Holloway, a distinguished professor of materials science and engineering and the project's lead researcher. Holloway and several colleagues at UF have received more than $400,000 for the first phase of the research from DARPA. The project is only a little over a year old, but the researchers have applied for several patents for their findings and plan scientific publication of their work.

Holloway observes that today's smart weapons rely on systems that use refractive optics, or lenses that bend light, to produce a focused view of the target. The resulting image is like that seen through a telescope—the view of the target is good but the surroundings are completely lost. This limits a weapon's accuracy on moving targets, as well as its ability to overcome flares or other countermeasures designed to confuse the weapon. Refractive systems also are relatively heavy, because they use mechanical systems to move the lens and keep the target in view. In addition, according to Holloway, the added weight requires more propellant and increased size, which boosts the cost.

The alternative approach taken by Holloway's team of engineers and physicists relies on diffractive optics, which uses interference effects to redirect light in different directions instead of bending it as today's smart weapons do. Their vision for the technology merges the developments of a nineteenth-century French physicist named Augustin Fresnel with a modern appreciation of how insect eyes work. Fresnel invented the Fresnel zone plate, also known as the Fresnel lens, which uses concentric circles of transparent and opaque material to diffract light into a single, marginally focused beam. The Fresnel lens became the standard on lighthouses for many years.

Holloway and his colleagues have modified the zone plate, replacing the transparent rings with a series of precisely spaced holes that sharpen the focus quality of the beam. Although similar devices, called photon sieves, have been around since 2001, they are typically used for X-rays or other electromagnetic radiation outside the visible light spectrum.

The UF team is the first to develop photon sieves for visible and longer-wavelength light, including infrared light, Holloway reports. The latter can have important implications for weaponized vision systems, which sometimes use infrared light. Art Hebard, a UF physicist and member of the project team, says that although the holes help sharpen the focus of the light, they also significantly reduce the amount of light that gets through the metal plate, which can degrade sensitivity. He and his colleagues are developing a way to combat this by adapting another physical phenomenon: surface plasmons, which occur when light strikes a metal surface, such as silver. The light generates electrical charge oscillations, called surface plasmons.

Hebard says the UF team has made progress in reconverting these plasmons into light by altering the surface characteristics of the metal. He points out that "If you can corrugate or structure the metal properly, you can reconvert plasmons back into light, [and by doing so] you get increased transmission of light because some of the light that is hitting the opaque part of the lens is transmitted rather than absorbed." More light transmission means better overall vision.

The team has made and tested small prototypes of the lenses. Once perfected, the next step could be to put many such lenses together—some designed for high resolution, others for lower resolution—onto a surface to produce a multiple-eye effect. The result, according to Holloway, would be a lightweight panoramic vision device with no moving parts.

Leonard J. Buckley, a program manager in materials chemistry at DARPA's Defense Science Office, says the technology is promising. "[It] has the potential to change the way we think about optics and specifically about optical lenses," he says. "Inspiration from nature has enabled the pursuit of new materials approaches to optical components, which will allow more lifelike qualities in the system."

Smart weapons aren't the only potential application. Robots designed to operate autonomously—such as those used to transport nuclear materials, fight oil well fires, or do other tasks too dangerous for people—also could benefit from improved vision systems, according to Buckley. Eventually, such lenses may even replace refractive lenses in consumer products, such as cameras, making them lighter and potentially less costly.

BEE-INSPIRED ROBOTS: FIGHTING MACHINES OF THE FUTURE

Automated analysis of bee behavior may yield better robots, potentially paving the way for mobile fighting machines that could do much of the work—and assume most of the risk—currently shouldered by troops.

A new computer vision system for automated analysis of animal movement—honeybee activities, in particular—has implications for biologically inspired design of robots and computers. The animal movement analysis system is part of the BioTracking Project, an effort conducted by Georgia Institute of Technology robotics researchers led by Tucker Balch, an assistant professor of computing.

"We believe the language of behavior is common between robots and animals," Balch says. "That means, potentially, that we could videotape ants for a long period of time, learn their 'program' and run it on a robot." Social insects, such as ants and bees, represent successful large-scale, robust behavior forged from the interaction of many, simple individuals, Balch explains. Such behavior can offer ideas on how to organize a cooperating colony of robots capable of complex operations.

To expedite the understanding of such behavior, Balch's team developed a computer vision system that automates analysis of animal movement—once an arduous and time-consuming task. Researchers are using the system to analyze data on the sequential movements that encode information; for example, how bees locate distant food sources.

With an 81.5 percent accuracy rate, the system can automatically analyze bee movements and label them based on examples provided by human experts. This level of accuracy is high enough to allow researchers to build a new system to determine the behavior of a bee from its sequence of motions, Balch notes.

For example, one sequence of commonly performed bee motions are waggle dances, which consist of arcing to the right, waggling (walking in a generally straight line while oscillating left and right), arcing to the left, waggling, and so on. These motions encode the locations of distant food sources, according to Cornell University professor of biology Thomas Seeley, who has collaborated with Balch on this project. Balch is also working with Professor Deborah Gordon of Stanford University on related work with ants.

Balch's animal movement analysis system has several components. First, researchers videotape bees for about 15 minutes, some of which are marked with a bright-colored paint and returned to the observation hive. Then computer vision-based tracking software converts the video of the marked bees into x- and y-coordinate location information for each animal in each frame of the footage. Some segments of this data are hand labeled by a researcher and then used as motion examples for the automated analysis system.

In future work, Balch and his colleagues will build a system that can learn executable models of these behaviors and then run the models in simulation. These simulations, Balch explains, would reveal the accuracy of the models. Researchers don't yet know if these models will yield better computer programming algorithms, though they are hopeful based on what previous research has revealed.

"Computer scientists have applied some of the algorithms discovered by biologists working with insects to challenging problems in computing," Balch says. "One example is network routing, which dictates the path data takes across the Internet. In this case the insect-based network routing algorithm, investigated by Marco Dorigo, is the best solution to date." But challenges lie ahead for the researchers. They will have to grapple with differences between the motor and sensory capabilities of robots and insects, according to Balch.

In related research with Professor Kim Wallen at Emory University's Yerkes National Primate Research Center, Balch and team member Zia Khan are observing monkeys with a similar computer vision system. They hope these studies will yield behavior models that can be implemented in computer code. The research team is learning about the spatial memory of, and social interaction among, monkeys. Already, they can track the movements of individual monkeys as they search for and find hidden treats in a large enclosure. Later, they want to observe a troop of sixty to eighty monkeys living together in a larger compound.

So far, researchers have learned that male and female monkeys have different spatial memories. Males apparently remember the physical distance to food, while females follow landmarks to find treats, Balch says.

"We . . . measure precisely where the monkeys go and how long it takes them to find the food," Balch explains. "We use the information from experiments to test hypotheses on spatial memory. We're more interested in the social systems among these animals. But we need this basic capability to track monkeys in 3D. So this work is a first step in this direction."

Ultimately, Balch and his colleagues in the Georgia Tech College of Computing's "Borg Lab"—named after the Borg of "Star Trek" fame—want to use this animal behavior information to design robots that work effectively with people in dynamic, noisy, and unknown environments such as those faced by military units.

THE NEW ALCHEMY: BIO-FUEL FOR MISSILES

The Office of Naval Research is hoping that one-celled organisms will reduce the costs of producing a missile propellant. With funding from the ONR's Green Synthesis of Energetic Materials program, microbiologist John Frost and his team at Michigan State University have created strains of microbes that convert certain types of sugars into a nonnatural synthetic material, called butanetriol. The navy depends on the slightly yellow liquid to produce the propellant BTTN (butanetriol trinitrate), which is used in some missiles, including the Hellfire.

Biologist and ONR program officer Harold Bright initiated the green project 3 years ago when he learned that chemists at the Navy Surface Warfare Center in Indian Head, Maryland, couldn't afford adequate supplies of chemically produced butanetriol. To fill the gap they use nitroglycerin, which is less expensive but more sensitive to physical shocks and temperature changes.

Currently, butanetriol costs $30 to $40 per pound, and together the navy and army purchase about 15,000 pounds per year. If the costs could be reduced to $10 or $15 per pound, Indian Head estimates the services' demand could rise to 180,000 pounds per year, replacing nitroglycerin in a number of current and new applications.

Bright adds, "This is a biology-unique process that in terms of environmental cleanliness and costs, chemists cannot match. Eventually, this 'green' production method will be applied to other materials, as we move away from petroleum-based processes that are environmentally 'dirty' and therefore expensive."

The researchers at Michigan State were able to manipulate the DNA of *Escherichia coli* and *Pseudomonas fragi* bacteria so that they would act like mini-factories, spewing out butanetriol as they go about their normal life functions. This process is "at the cutting edge of both civilian and military science," explains Bright.

In contrast to the high-pressure, high-temperature chemical process to produce butanetriol, the microbes require only air, sugar, and salts in a warm water environment. Once they've produced the butanetriol and lived out their lives, they are killed and then disposed of in a standard municipal sewage treatment facility.

ROBOTIC SENSORS: HIDDEN TARGET DETECTORS

A vision of futuristic robotic aircraft and land vehicles that can sense and close in on targets hidden in trees, caves, or bunkers is being explored by a new four-university research initiative. The hunt would begin over a wide area, using stationary and moving sensors that might scan for communications signals emanating from a bunker, or the different kinds of electromagnetic signatures put out by machinery, or the infrared waves emitted by a heated

object. Other sensors, perhaps installed aboard airborne or surface
vehicles, would autonomously coordinate their activities with minimal intervention from humans. They would narrow down the
search for a given target by using complex mathematical formulas
to locate the "fields" in space where the telltale waves vibrate.
"The idea of doing multisensing on multiple unmanned platforms
is new," says Lawrence Carin, a professor of electrical and computer engineering at Duke University, who is leading the effort. "It
hasn't been done before. Almost everything we have proposed is
new." The technology being developed would allow increasingly
localized sensor searches for quarry so hidden that "you don't
even know where to start to look without this technology," Carin
says. "This is a very challenging problem. It will constitute a big
leap ahead from where things are today."

Researchers at Duke, Georgia Institute of Technology, Stanford University, and the University of Michigan will each take on
different parts of developing the enabling mathematical underpin-
nings of this technology with $6 million in DARPA funding, which
will be administered through the U.S. Army over 5 years. The
objective, according to the language of the award, is the development of "detection and classification algorithms for multimodal
inverse problems." That means developing mathematical rules—
called algorithms—to train and control multiple sensors that, with
increasing precision, could detect invisible signals emanating from
such targets, and trace those signals back to their sources (a technique called inversion). "The targets could be land mines, targets
under trees like tanks or troops, or targets in underground bunkers
or caves," says Carin, the overall administrator of the DARPA Multi-
University Research Initiative (MURI) grant to Duke, Georgia Tech,
and Stanford. The Michigan work, while funded separately, is
being coordinated with the MURI project.

Once potential targets are perceived, the search might be pin-
pointed using a different mix of sensors. "For instance, if vehicles
are moving through trees, you could actually sense the motion,"
he adds. "A hole in the ground will cause perturbation to the gravity that's observed on the surface, so you can detect that." Other
sensors, he notes, might register acoustic vibrations. These arrays

would do more than just sense passively; they would also *infer* from these different signals what their sources are through the inversion process. "In the campaign in Afghanistan, they're using a lot of unmanned Predator drone aircraft," Carin points out. "Our vision is that in the future you could have multiple drones out there, not just collecting data but actually doing the inversion."

Internal control is important. According to Carin, "You would like them to be self-controlled," which means they would not need detailed updating to tell them what to do after being sent out to a certain area. "They would make decisions on their own," he says. "A sensor would have to be able to think. You could have multiple drones and multiple land robots that communicate with one another and do the inversion on the fly, because it is too complicated for them to communicate back to their controllers, and moreover through communications traffic they will reveal themselves," Carin says.

What would happen with several robots? "Let's say they are sensing for electromagnetic radiation due to traffic or machinery," says Carin. "Let's assume they sense something interesting. They may then turn on a seismic sensor or gravity sensor. As they learn information, that [information] will guide how [they] use other sensors."

This project builds on a previous one, also directed by Carin, which coordinated research into land-mine detection performed by investigators at Duke, Georgia Tech, Stanford, California Institute of Technology, and Ohio State University. The earlier work means the new team members have a considerable track record working with inversions algorithms that deal with both "noisy" field data and "a multiplicity of sensors and applications," Carin notes. "Our inversion algorithms now represent the state of the art in this field and are deployed in systems being developed for the Army Countermine Office," he states. In the process of that research, which still continues through separate grants, "we developed a close working relationship with the Army Night Vision Laboratory and associated contractors."

Waymond Scott, an electrical and computer engineering professor at Georgia Tech and a top expert on the effects of vibrations on soils and buried objects, is a key researcher on the team and was also involved in the previous MURI project. Scott's work will focus on detecting obscured structures, such as buried land mines, with seismic and electromagnetic waves. His approach will combine both experiment and theory. "Our major emphasis is [to understand] the physics of how these waves interact so we can design better sensors, improve signal processing algorithms, and put some bounds on what will be practical in sensing systems," Scott says. "We will also have a strong coupling between our experimental work and our numerical modeling efforts. Having better models will help us understand the complexities of the sensors."

He notes that detection of buried land mines and underground structures such as tunnels or bunkers is made more difficult because soil, unlike air or water, is not a homogeneous material. Layers of different soil types, and objects such as rocks and sticks, affect the transmissions of waves. As a result, complicated analysis techniques are needed to pick out the targets. In past work, Scott and his Georgia Tech collaborators have been successful in detecting unique resonances created by land mines and the complicated mechanical structures inside them.

Stanford mathematician George Papanicolau will work on reverse time migration, a method to measure invisible waves, forces, or vibrations and, in effect, "reverse them in time" so they lead back to their sources. Alfred Hero, a professor of electrical engineering and computer science, will lead the development of new statistical signal processing and classification algorithms at the University of Michigan.

SOLDIER'S PROTECTOR: HANDHELD WEAPON-SNIFFING SENSOR

Soldiers suspicious that a truck or box may contain explosives or chemical weapons may soon be able to find out for sure by shooting the target with a sticky little projectile that can detect the danger and report it from afar. That's certainly a big improvement over today's most often used approach: manual inspection.

The crayon-size sensor, which is fired from a standard paintball gun, was invented by a team of University of Florida undergraduate engineering students as part of a government- and corporate-supported engineering research and education program. Lockheed Martin's Orlando-based Missiles and Fire Control, which sponsored the project, plans to refine the projectile and put it into production.

Leslie Kramer, director and engineering fellow for Missiles and Fire Control, says the sensor would be an ideal tool for identifying improvised explosive devices (IEDs)—disguised homemade bombs that have injured and killed scores in Iraq. "These IEDs—a lot of these things are being buried in piles of trash—[but] if you had a good chemical sensor on this projectile, you could fire it into the trash and stand back and determine [if] it detect[ed] TNT leaking out of an artillery shell."

Guided by mechanical and aerospace engineering professor Loc Vu-Quoc, a team of six engineering seniors designed and built the projectile over the course of the year-long Integrated Product and Process Design, or IPPD, program. It was a challenge: Lockheed officials outlined what they wanted in broad terms and told the students to be creative. The team, which included students from several different engineering fields, considered numerous approaches, including a gun made of plastic tubing, before deciding to try an off-the-shelf paintball gun shooting a modified projectile.

The team built a tiny circuit board containing a transmitter, sensor, and wire antenna, all powered by a watch battery. They inserted the circuit board in a cylindrical case tipped with the sticky industrial polymer. The weight of the polymer, together with the arrangement of the components, causes the projectile to be heaviest at the front, which helps it fly straight and strike the target with its sticky end. "What we did was we made its tip heavy so it's like a dart—it doesn't tumble over," says electrical engineering student Felipe Sutantri.

Chemical and explosive detectors are expensive and difficult to work with, so the team tested their prototype using a tiny accelerometer, a sensor that registers movement. Accelerometers are commonly used in air bags to sense collisions. In a variety of tests, the team showed the accelerometers and other electronics could survive being shot out of the gun and striking a target. They were able to measure the accelerometer's data remotely at impact using oscilloscopes and laptop computers, much the way laptop-equipped soldiers might glean information from a deployed version of the projectile on the battlefield. "I think the most important thing for the proof of concept was to see if the electronics could survive the impact," Sutantri says.

The students' tests proved the transmitter could report data from up to 240 feet from the laptop, while the paintball gun could shoot the projectile at least 65 feet. Both distances could be extended in the production version, and engineers also likely will shrink the projectile's size and weight. "The next step is the integration of other detectors into this projectile and also modifying what the students did to make it more tactical," Kramer says.

GAIT RECOGNITION: THE WAY YOU WALK

How you walk may not be as distinctive as John Wayne's swagger or the sashay of Joan Collins, but your stride may still be unique enough to identify you at a distance—alone or among a group of people. Researchers at the Georgia Institute of Technology and elsewhere are developing technologies to recognize a person's walk, or gait. Results indicate these new identification methods hold promise as tools in the war on terrorism and in medical diagnosis.

Gait recognition technology is a biometric method, that is, a unique biological or behavioral identification characteristic, such as a fingerprint or a face. Though still in its infancy, the technology is growing in significance because of federal studies, such as the Georgia Tech projects. At Georgia Tech, one study is addressing issues of gait recognition by computer vision, and the other is exploring a novel approach—gait recognition with a radar system similar to those used by police officers to catch speeders.

The ultimate goal is to detect, classify, and identify humans at distances of up to 500 feet under all-weather conditions, day or night. Such capabilities will enhance the protection of U.S. forces and facilities from terrorist attacks, according to federal officials. "We need technology to find the bad guys at a distance," says Jon Geisheimer, a research engineer at the Georgia Tech Research Institute (GTRI).

Because gait recognition technology is so new, researchers are assessing the uniqueness of gait and methods by which it can be evaluated. "We know that we can get some information on gait, but that it is much less diagnostic than faces," says Aaron Bobick, an associate professor of computing and codirector of the computer vision project at Georgia Tech. "Currently, we can't recognize 1 in 100,000 people. At the moment, gait recognition is not capable of that, but it's getting better so it can act as a filter."

In its early development, gait recognition technology likely will serve as a screening tool in conjunction with other biometric methods. With 2 years of experiments and analysis almost complete, researchers on both Georgia Tech projects are hopeful for continued funding to conduct further studies. They must address numerous technical issues, and it will be at least 5 years before the technologies are commercially available, researchers say.

In the project using radar for gait recognition, results from experiments, data analysis, and algorithm design are promising, says Geisheimer. Gait recognition by radar focuses on the gait cycle formed by the movements of a person's various body parts over time. "The magic goal we're shooting for is accuracy in the high 90 percent range," Geisheimer says. "We're not there yet, but our initial results are encouraging and promising." Researchers correctly identified 80 to 95 percent of individual subjects, with variances in that range, during 3 days of experiments. The next step is to build a more powerful radar system and test it in the lab and then the field. In experiments last year, subjects started walking 50 feet away from the radar and then walked within 15 feet of it; still a far cry from the goal of 500 or more feet.

In the study of gait recognition by computer vision, researchers distinguish their approach from others with a technique called an activity-specific static biometric. A static property—for example, a person's leg length—is not a property of motion itself. It can be measured from a single image. "The advantage of measuring a static property is that it is amenable to being done from multiple viewpoints," Bobick says. "Static measurements are view invariant, and that is a tremendous advantage because you can't control where someone goes."

Researchers are also developing statistical analysis tools for using a small, easily gathered database to predict how well a particular biometric, including gait recognition, will work on a larger population. These techniques will also help researchers determine what gait recognition properties to measure based on how well the technology can measure them. "You can work on your ability to improve measurements," Bobick says. "But if you're not measuring something that is diagnostic, there is no amount of technology that will solve that problem with the biometric."

Still in its infancy, computer vision-based gait recognition technology holds promise, particularly for verification or screening, if it is used in conjunction with other biometric technologies and information, Bobick predicts. Meanwhile, researchers are applying the findings from their studies funded by DARPA to ongoing research in understanding human movement through video.

CHAPTER TWO

THE FINGERTIPS WAR

INFORMATION SYSTEMS

INFORMATION AT YOUR FINGERTIPS is vital for business, of course. But for the military, fast, reliable information is often a matter of life or death. That is because obtaining data on factors such as troop movements, local terrain, weather, and available resources can decide battlefield success or failure. Increasingly, "fingertips information" is revolutionizing warfare.

Most people believe that modern information systems technology—the processing of information by computer—came about because business needed a cheaper and easier way to bill customers, track inventory, manage payrolls, and so on. Not true.

While electronic computers have certainly revolutionized business, they were initially developed to meet the needs of war—specifically, World War II. Early computers, such as Colossus and the Harvard Mark I, helped Allied leaders break enemy codes, project artillery shell trajectories, plot ship courses, and handle a variety of other time-critical computations. It was these systems that laid the foundation for the development of the first high-powered business-oriented machines in the late 1940s and early 1950s.

Computers are as vital to today's military as bullets and bombs. Modern computers, which can be as small as a single chip, control everything from jet fighters to trucks. They can track the movements of friendly and enemy troops, supplies, weapons, and the weather. In the years ahead, computers will become even more useful, controlling, tracking, and managing an ever greater number of systems and devices. Artificial intelligence (AI) will help eliminate much of the grunt work that consumes time and resources, and will also allow computers to advise military leaders on various battle scenarios and options.

BRINGING BANDWIDTH
TO THE BATTLEFIELD

Anyone who is involved in information technology will tell you that integrating different software packages is notoriously tough. There are lots of unintended consequences when you try to run different applications together—and even hardware like PCs can break. If you work in a large enough company, you call the help desk, but what if you're a combat sailor or a marine in the front lines? How can navy warships and marine riflemen use the American information advantage in the wet, mucky, and dangerous arena that is their workplace?

Ultimately, the men and women who defend freedom will need:

- A long-haul network for command, control, communications, and intelligence.

- Knowledge-management tools that help them understand and act in concert on information they receive.

- Wireless technologies that give them the bandwidth they need in the field.

These are essential components of the navy's new concept called FORCEnet (network for forces). When fully operational, FORCEnet will provide the operational construct and architectural framework for naval warfare in the information age, integrating personnel, sensors, command and control, platforms, and weapons into a networked, distributed combat force. Its aligned and integrated systems, functions, and missions will substantially increase combat capabilities. The goal is to transform situational awareness, accelerate the speed of decision making, and allow for greatly distributed combat power. Once in place, FORCEnet will harness information for knowledge-based combat operations and, it is hoped, increase force survivability.

The Office of Naval Research (ONR) has taken the lead on creating the scientific and technological foundation for the information architecture that will serve Sea Power 21, the navy's new operational system, which employs information superiority to deliver unprecedented offensive power, defensive assurance, and operational independence. ONR has teamed with the navy's system commands to provide real war-fighting benefits now, while at the same time drafting a roadmap to the future.

A variety of intelligent agents (specialized computer programs that select and present important data) and the software architectures these agents need in order to work well together make up the knowledge-management part of FORCEnet. Together they will help sailors and marines separate the important information from the trivia. The ramifications are clearly enormous, since obviously if you don't manage information well in combat you'll find that you've replaced the fog of war with the glare of war.

The Advanced Multi-Function Radio Frequency Concept (AMRF-C), one of the most technologically challenging and revolutionary steps in the road toward fully implementing FORCEnet, is rapidly moving ahead in shore-based demonstrations. In addition, new antenna technologies being developed through the ONR's AMRF-C project will eliminate the interference plaguing the antenna farms that sprout on ships and around command posts.

The FORCEnet concept was a product of several years' work by the navy's Strategic Studies Group, a forum of savvy officers with plenty of fleet experience. It aimed at bringing the navy's concept of network-centric warfare (warfare focused on network technology) to reality. Chief of Naval Operations Admiral Vern Clark has decided to accelerate FORCEnet for early delivery.

"FORCEnet isn't another big-think 'vision' that generates more PowerPoint than combat power," says ONR's Bobby Junker. "JTF

WARNET, which was built with fielded systems, has already been demonstrated and is being deployed."

AIDE-DE-CAMP: A COGNITIVE SOFTWARE HELPER

Researchers at Carnegie Mellon University's School of Computer Science (SCS) have embarked on a 5-year project to develop a software-based cognitive personal assistant that will help people—including military leaders—improve their work productivity. The researchers believe the new technology will be equally valuable to managers in industry, academia, government, and the military.

The Reflective Agents with Distributed Adaptive Reasoning (RADAR) project aims to help users handle tasks such as scheduling meetings, allocating resources, creating coherent reports from snippets of information, and managing e-mail by grouping related messages, flagging high-priority requests, and automatically proposing answers to routine messages.

The goal is to develop a system that can both save time for its user and improve the quality of decisions. RADAR will handle some routine tasks by itself, ask for confirmation on others, and produce suggestions and drafts that its user can modify as needed. Over time, the system must learn when and how often to interrupt its busy user with questions and suggestions. To accomplish all this, the RADAR research team must employ techniques from a variety of fields, including machine learning, human–computer interaction, natural language processing, flexible planning, and behavioral studies of human managers.

The RADAR project's principal investigators include SCS professors Daniel P. Siewiorek, director of Carnegie Mellon's Human–Computer Interaction Institute; Jaime Carbonell, director of the Language Technologies Institute; and principal research computer scientist Scott Fahlman. The project will initially focus on four tasks to illustrate how the system's learning curve increases people's productivity: e-mail, scheduling, webmaster, and space planning. "With each task, we'll run experiments to see how well people do by themselves and make comparisons," says Siewiorek. The researchers will also compare individuals working with a human assistant to those using the software agent.

Besides working on these four specific tasks, the project will develop cross-cutting technologies that can be used in all of these tasks and in other personal-assistant tasks as well. These include a shared knowledge base, a module that decides when to interrupt the user with questions, and a module that extracts information such as meeting requests from e-mail messages written in English.

"The key scientific challenge in this work is to endow RADAR with enough flexibility and general knowledge to handle tasks of this nature," says Fahlman. Like any good assistant, RADAR must understand its human master's activities and preferences and how they change over time. RADAR must respond to specific instructions (i.e., "Notify me as soon as the new budget numbers arrive by e-mail"—without the need for reprogramming). "But the system also must be able to learn by interacting with its master to see how he or she reacts to various events. It must know when to interrupt its master with a question and when to defer," says Fahlman.

The research team has received an initial $7 million in funding from the Defense Advanced Research Projects Agency (DARPA).

THE END OF BATTLE FATIGUE: COPING WITH INFORMATION OVERLOAD

One of the key problems military leaders face in this era of ubiquitous information access is information overload. For leaders attempting to make on-the-spot, life-and-death judgments, an overabundance of information can be almost as decision-crippling as having no information at all.

Recognizing this problem, Penn State University researchers have developed new software that can help decision-making teams in combat situations or homeland security handle information overload by inferring teams' information needs and delivering relevant data from computer-generated reports.

The agent software, called Collaborative Agents for Simulating Teamwork (CAST), highlights relevant data. This helps improve a team's decision-making process and also enhances members' collaboration. "This version of CAST provides support for teams by anticipating what information team members will need, finding commonalities in the available information, and determining how that information should be processed," says John Yen, professor of information sciences and technology. "Decision making is made easier because the software offers only relevant data."

CAST was originally developed by a team of researchers at Texas A&M where Yen was a key figure. Now a faculty member in Penn State's School of Information Sciences and Technology (IST), Yen heads the Research Laboratory for Team-Based Agents at the university while continuing to collaborate with Richard Volz and Michael Miller, from Texas A&M, on the software.

Initially, CAST was developed to facilitate or train human teams in the best ways to collaborate on and perform certain tasks. The research has been funded through a Department of Defense MURI (Multidisciplinary Research Program of the University Research Initiative) grant to Texas A&M, Wright State University, and Penn State.

With this research, they are taking smart software into a new direction involving what Yen calls "shared mental models" to support team activities or to train teams. These can include shared team goals, shared assumptions about the problem, and shared knowledge about the team structure and process. "The inspiration came from psychologists studying the behavior of human teams who were required to process incoming information under the pressure of time constraints," Yen says.

Without receiving directions, members of higher-performing teams were able to provide each other with needed information, which enabled more timely and better decisions, according to Yen. CAST does this, too. "The more time-critical the environment in which a team operates, the more effectively it needs to process information," Yen says. "A computer program that acts as a team member may be more efficient in processing information than a human teammate."

The Penn State researcher and his collaborators see CAST as a promising technology for supporting military officers who receive as many as 600,000 reports every hour from ground sensors and satellites. Without the right information, the wrong decision can be made in the battle space, notes Yen.

The software, which can be customized, also can help officers adapt more quickly to changing battlefield conditions. CAST also could be used to track potential terrorist threats or infectious diseases; indeed, it would have application wherever information needs to be exchanged quickly or commonalities found among different things, events, situations, and so on.

BATTLE BLOG

Blogging, the practice of keeping a weblog or a blog, is typically seen as a solitary, even narcissistic activity. An individual can type frequent updates onto their log, sharing opinions or ideas with anyone accessing the Internet. Today, the ONR and the Naval Undersea Warfare Center (NUWC) are testing the idea that weblogs can be powerful communication tools bringing together teams of people. If it succeeds, it could have important military applications, and the future of blogging could be very different from what it is today.

The ONR and NUWC are leading a government-industry team to develop the blog's promising new approach to speed up the exchange of information on new defense technologies, thereby getting the technologies into the field more quickly. A pilot blog is being developed by Providence, Rhode Island–based Traction Software, a company that specializes in the development of enterprise blogs designed for corporations and other major organizations. The system will serve as a medium for the distribution of general information to staffers from the seven team members. It also will enable users to post proprietary data, such as test results and reports that are accessible only to designated readers. The blog's home page will resemble a newspaper consisting of stories posted by users.

The first military program to use blog technology is a team evaluating a night-vision technology developed by Ford Motor Corporation. The team members include Ford, the Marine Corps, the Army's Night Vision Lab, the Defense Acquisition University, and the New York Police Department. Using blog technology, the researchers can propose new features, comment on various concepts, alert others to relevant breaking news, and generally participate in an open exchange of ideas and opinions.

SELF-HEALING DATABASES

Innovative new software can detect and correct a database impaired by an attack while the database system continues to process transactions. "We simulated attackers' behaviors on a database and then monitored the response of the database," says Peng Liu, assistant professor of information sciences and technology at Penn State. "We can't prevent attackers from getting in, but with this technology, the database can heal itself on-the-fly."

Liu performed the research underlying the technology while a faculty member at the University of Maryland. He has since established his research team, the Cyber Security Group, in Penn State's School of Information Sciences and Technology. The team's areas of expertise include network security, intrusion detection and masking, survivable systems, and attack prediction.

All databases are vulnerable to being breached by unauthorized users or hackers looking for a challenge. With more databases than ever, experts expect the number of database attacks to continue to rise. For the military, that leaves at risk such data-intensive applications as troop organization and deployment, materiel, air-traffic control, naval vessel deployment, and various other command-and-control systems. Although many intrusions can be detected soon after the database is breached, the damage usually doesn't stop with the initial transaction. Subsequent transactions and data updating can spread the damage.

Existing recovery software creates its own problems. Rolling back activity to the initial damage is expensive because the work of many unaffected transactions by good users will be lost, Liu says. For commercial databases, suspending the database to clean up the damage is undesirable and, in many cases, unacceptable. International banks, for instance, need 24-7 access to account data.

The family of algorithms developed by Liu and others can detect single, multiple, or simultaneous attacks. But it does more. It isolates malicious transactions, so that many benign ones are preserved from being affected and having to be re-executed. It also repairs the database by containing the set of corrupted data objects and then undoing or unwinding the direct and indirect effects of the attack.

The technology has another advantage: The software can be adapted for static and on-the-fly repairs. Because it's dynamic, new transactions can continue even while the database is being repaired. Furthermore, the new technology is intelligent and adaptive. "The database can adapt its own behavior and reconfigure itself based on the attack," says Liu. In addition to safeguarding databases from individual hackers, the technology could also protect vulnerable systems from a coordinated enemy cyber-attack. A prototype of the attack-resilient software is being tested by the Cyber Security Group and the U.S. Air Force.

WHEN IT HAS TO GET THERE: RADIO FREQUENCY IDENTIFICATION

Information never before obtained about supplies and equipment will be available to the military through the next generation of Radio Frequency Identification (RFID) technology known as Auto-ID.

The Department of Defense Combat Feeding Directorate, at the U.S. Army Soldier Systems Center in Natick, Massachusetts, has joined nearly 100 companies and 5 international research universities as sponsors of the Auto-ID Center at the Massachusetts Institute of Technology (MIT).

The center, founded in 1999, is developing technology based on nonproprietary, global standards that will create an affordable solution for the Defense Department and commercial industry worldwide. Combat Feeding calls this initiative Global Asset Visibility. "The global supply chain is a bigger network than most people realize," says Kathy Evangelos, executive assistant to the Combat Feeding director. "Auto-ID will automate the global supply chain."

The Universal Product Code (UPC), a bar code of lines and numbers now used to identify objects, has existed since the 1970s for logistics management, but the technology is limited. During Operation Desert Storm, the military did not know what was in 25,000 of the 40,000 containers sent overseas, according to Evangelos. Containers today can be tracked with RFID tags, and they have greatly improved the situation for operations Enduring Freedom and Iraqi Freedom. Still, Auto-ID offers more. "We're starting to see tags with microchips in all kinds of products," says Evangelos. "Industry sees RFID as a replacement for the bar code, and Auto-ID takes it a step further."

The technology is based on the Electronic Product Code (EPC), a 96-bit code capable of identifying more than 80 thousand trillion, trillion unique items. An electronic tag containing an EPC on a microchip wirelessly stores and transmits data to a reader. The EPC code serves as an address directing users to an Internet site where managed levels of information on the item are found.

Information retrieval is possible using the Object Naming Service, which associates the EPC with an item. It points to a server that uses the Physical Mark-Up Language to distribute and represent related information, such as shipping instructions, inspection schedules, location, expiration dates, or even technical manuals. Savant software technology manages the flow of data and provides an interface to legacy systems.

Auto-ID will provide real-time visibility. Accurate automated inventories will eliminate the need for manual counts, according to Evangelos, which ultimately reduces the supply-chain footprint and associated costs. Furthermore, EPC tags will allow automatic manifests to be written to containers, and sensor integration will provide the capability to monitor the status of an item, pallet, or container by detecting variables such as temperature, vibration, rough handling, or chemical or biological contamination that could affect product quality. "Initially we want to track rations, but imagine what it can do for vaccines and other medical supplies and other temperature-sensitive items," says Evangelos.

One potential Auto-ID application is reading a temperature profile from a container or pallet tag that translates complicated data using a shelf-life model, developed by MIT for Combat Feeding. The model will allow food inspectors to determine the condition of Meals, Ready-to-Eat or Unitized Group Rations, using a simple, easy-to-understand color-coded system: green for "issue," yellow for "limited inspection," and red for "100 percent inspection."

Corporations plan to track down to the item level such things as packages of disposable razor blades or bottles of laundry detergent, but Combat Feeding is interested in tracking at the case, pallet, and container level. Case level or Type 1 passive tags come in various shapes and sizes and cost anywhere from 20 cents to $1. Eventually, these tags will cost less than $0.05. Pallet and container or Type 3 battery tags today cost as much as $150. "The tags we are testing currently cost around $17, and eventually revolutionary technology advancements using tiny NanoBlocks will bring the cost down to $1 to make widespread use affordable," says Evangelos.

Combat Feeding is currently evaluating Auto-ID's potential for automatic, real-time tracking and visibility at the supply points; automatic inventories to units issued; capturing historical product temperature data; and automatic tracking and updates of container inventories. The results obtained from this research will help set the framework for a proposed Defense Logistics Agency Advanced Concept Technology Demonstration (ACTD), scheduled in 2005. Although combat rations are the demonstration product, any military item, including ammunition and spare parts for vehicles, can be tracked under the program to help soldiers ultimately get what they need when they need it.

PORTABLE POWER AND ATOMIC BATTERIES

On the battlefield, a reliable source of power to operate the many advanced electronic devices a soldier carries is essential, but today's heavy and cumbersome batteries fall short in satisfying the military's needs.

In search of both a lightweight and reliable alternative, the Department of Energy's Pacific Northwest National Laboratory (PNNL) has developed the smallest power system yet, all wrapped up in a micro-size package.

PNNL researchers, with funding from DARPA, have developed the world's smallest catalytic fuel processing reactor system. The technology aims to provide a low-watt power source for handheld wireless equipment, sensors, and other small but essential devices required by today's troops.

The petite power system—about the size of a cigarette lighter—converts liquid fuel to electricity via a micro-scale fuel processor coupled with a miniature fuel cell developed by Case Western Reserve University. An integral part of the system is PNNL's fuel reformer, about the size of a pencil eraser, which enables the system to convert fuel and water into hydrogen-rich gas. The fuel cell then generates electricity by converting hydrogen and oxygen from the air into electrical power and clean water.

"Our miniaturized fuel processor incorporates several chemical processes and operations in one device," says Evan Jones, PNNL's principal investigator. The fuel processor system contains two vaporizers, a heat exchanger, a catalytic combustor, and a steam reformer, all within a compact package no larger than a dime.

The military envisions many useful applications for this emerging miniaturized energy-generating technology. According to Terry Doherty, director of PNNL's DoD programs, soldiers could power personal, lightweight cooling systems while wearing protective suits and gear, prolonging their own comfort and efficiency during a reconnaissance.

"Vital personal communications devices could function for extended periods without the added weight of bulky, inefficient batteries," Doherty says. He adds that miniature sensors powered by the same technology could be scattered before advancing troops to monitor ground vibrations or detect dangerous toxic agents and relay this information electronically to soldiers. This technology broadens the possibilities for using self-sustaining items such as mobile devices in remote or difficult-to-access locations.

While methanol has proved to be the most effective fuel source, other liquid fuels such as butane, jet fuel—also known as JP-8—or even diesel may be used. And, because the hydrogen power source is produced only as needed, there is no need to store or carry the volatile gas, reducing risk and creating a lighter load.

Testing has revealed that performance from the reformer and fuel cell prototype is impressive. "This system can produce an equivalent power (20 mW) to batteries, but at one-third the weight," Jones says. Similar micro–fuel-cell systems with greater power output (50 W) currently under development are providing power equal to that of batteries weighing 10 times as much. Researchers suggest that with additional system efficiencies and improvements, even greater performance may be achievable.

PNNL researchers have found that huge processing plants, traditionally used to produce chemicals and other products, can be scaled down exponentially. "What can be achieved on a large scale," Jones says, "can be achieved at a micro-scale."

Meanwhile, at Cornell University researchers have built a microscopic device that could supply power for decades by drawing energy from a radioactive isotope. The device converts the energy stored in the radioactive material into motion. It could directly move the parts of a tiny machine or generate electricity in a form more useful for many circuits than has been possible with earlier devices. This new approach creates a high-impedance source (the factor that determines the amplitude of the current) better suited to power many types of circuits, according to Amit Lal, a Cornell assistant professor of electrical and computer engineering.

The prototype is the first MEMS (micro-electromechanical

FIGURE 2–1.   CORNELL ATOMIC BATTERY.

systems) version of a larger device that Lal, working with nuclear engineering professors James Blanchard and Douglas Henderson, designed and built while a member of the faculty at the University of Wisconsin—Madison.

The prototype (see Fig. 2–1) is made up of a copper strip 1 millimeter wide, 2 centimeters long, and 60 micrometers (millionths of a meter) thick that is cantilevered above a thin film of radioactive nickel-63 (an isotope of nickel with a different number of neutrons from the common form). (Future nanofabricated versions could be smaller than 1 cubic millimeter.) As the isotope decays, it emits beta particles (electrons). Radioactive materials can emit beta particles, alpha particles, or gamma rays, the last two of which can carry enough energy to be hazardous. Lal's device will use only isotopes that emit beta particles, whose energy is small enough not to penetrate skin.

The emitted electrons collect on the copper strip, building a negative charge, while the isotope film, losing electrons, becomes positively charged. The attraction between positive and negative bends the rod down and when the rod gets close enough to the isotope, a current flows, equalizing the charge. The rod springs up, and the process repeats. The principle is much like that underlying an electric doorbell, in which a moving bar alternately makes and breaks the electric circuit supplying the electromagnet that moves the bar.

Radioactive isotopes can continue to release energy over periods ranging from weeks to decades. The half-life of nickel-63, for example, is over 100 years, and, Lal says, a battery using this isotope might continue to supply useful energy for at least half that time. (Half-life is the time it takes for half the atoms in an element to decay.) Other isotopes offer varying combinations of energy level versus lifetime. Unlike chemical batteries, the devices will work in a very wide range of temperatures.

In addition to providing lightweight, long-lived power for an array of portable electronic devices, possible applications include sensors to monitor the condition of missiles stored in sealed containers, battlefield sensors that must be concealed and left unattended for long periods, and medical devices implanted inside the human body.

The moving cantilever can directly actuate a linear device or can move a cam or ratcheted wheel to produce rotary motion. A magnetized material attached to the rod can generate electricity as it moves through a coil. Lal has also built versions of the device in which the cantilever is made of a piezoelectric material that generates electricity when deformed, releasing a pulse of current as the rod snaps up. This also generates a radio-frequency pulse that could be used to transmit information. Alternatively, Lal suggests, the electrical pulse could drive a light-emitting diode to generate an optical signal.

In addition to powering other devices, the tiny cantilevers could be used as stand-alone sensors, Lal says. The devices ordinarily operate in a vacuum, but sensors might be developed to detect the presence or absence of particular gases, since introducing a gas to the device changes the flow of current between the rod and the base, in turn changing the period or amplitude of the oscillation. Temperature and pressure changes also can be detected. Lal and Cornell doctoral candidate Hang Guo are now building and testing practical sensors and power supplies based on this concept.

SHADOW ILLUMINATOR AND OTHER PHOTO-TWEAKING SOFTWARE

Carnegie Mellon University robotics researcher Vladimir Brajovic has developed a tool that automatically improves the appearance of darkened or underexposed photographs by digitally adding light to dark areas. The technology could lead to surveillance photographs that make visible those things that normally would appear invisible to the unaided human eye. These enhanced surveillance photographs, whether taken by people, satellites, planes, or security cameras, might then be able to provide valuable extra detail (such as aircraft tail numbers) or show objects that otherwise would have been missed.

The Shadow Illuminator was developed originally to help robots see better. Using principles based on the physics of how optical images are formed, Shadow Illuminator imitates the vision processes that take place in the human eye. It examines the content of a photograph, estimates the illumination conditions, and then brightens shadows. It also enhances details within the shadow. "Shadow Illuminator is intelligent and works consistently for all pictures," says Brajovic, director of the Computational Sensor Laboratory in Carnegie Mellon's Robotics Institute. "It provides the same results quickly and eliminates the hassle of manually adjusting photographs."

According to Brajovic, traditional image-enhancement tools manipulate the color and intensity of the pixels of an image regardless of its content, relying on human judgment to determine what parts of an image need adjustment. Applying this process to each image can be tedious and time consuming. "While there are other programs that enable users to manually produce similar results, you have to figure out what works for each individual picture," Brajovic says.

Another approach to image processing is being researched by Gemma Piella, a mathematician at the Polytechnical University of Catalonia's Telecommunications Engineering School, in Catalonia, Spain, who has developed a new method for processing images. This method allows more details to be visible at a lower resolution than the original image.

Piella uses a mathematical operation that makes use of "wavelets," mathematical algorithms that process data at different scales or resolutions. Wavelets only exist over a short distance, and all of the peaks and troughs have different heights and widths. These characteristics ensure that a single operation can simultaneously render both large and small objects visible. This enables viewers to see, in effect, both the entire forest and the individual trees at the same time.

A scene can only be fully understood if it can be seen at many different levels. For example, if you see a woodland from a distance, your first impression is just a green surface. If you move in closer, you can see the trees. If you zoom in even further still, you can see the leaves and the bark. Therefore, the information you extract from the picture depends upon the level from which it is viewed. So-called multiresolution techniques such as those used by Piella, render all details, from every level in the image visible at the same time.

By modifying existing wavelet techniques, Piella ensures that the wavelets make use of the geometrical information in the signal being processed. As a result, even the smallest details are clearly visible in images with a low resolution. For example, suppose an image contains smooth areas that are separated by pieces of crooked lines. Standard wavelets are good at isolating the start and end points of the crooked lines, but not in recognizing the trajectory of the line. Piella's modification allows the viewer to see that trajectory.

The mathematician also uses her innovative technique to combine different images of the same object into a single detailed image. This is important, for example, in medicine, where imaging techniques are used to visualize different aspects of the human body. For example, combining a CT scan and an MRI scan of the brain makes both the brain tissue and the bones visible. In sur-veillance photos, the technique could allow the viewer to see, for example, not only flatbed trucks, but the cargo that's stored on each truck's bed.

FROM HERE TO THERE AND THERE TO HERE

While "fingertips information" is revolutionizing warfare, equally important are the systems that move information from one place to another. After all, data that's stuck miles away from key decision makers is hardly "fingertips information." For this reason electronic supply lines in the form of wired and wireless networks and other advanced telecommunication technologies are playing an increasingly important role in today's military. We'll take a look at these systems, and their role in future combat, in Chapter 3.

CHAPTER THREE

EARLY WARNING

TELECOMMUNICATIONS, RECONNAISSANCE, AND DISASTER RELIEF

THE TERM, *FOG OF WAR,* is well known. In reality, the battlefield often *is* a foggy place: full of smoke, haze, dust, and noise. In past centuries, communication was limited by the distance soldiers and commanders could see and shout. During battle, this distance might be restricted to only a few feet, or even inches, by the ongoing pandemonium.

Radio broke the distance barrier in the early twentieth century, allowing communication to take place—first by telegraphy, then voice—over dozens, hundreds, and even thousands of miles. By the mid-twentieth century, radio had evolved to a level that allowed battlefield communication over almost any distance on virtually any type of terrain. By the century's end, radio equipment had become highly portable and satellites had filled in many of the gaps left open by terrestrial communications systems.

The twenty-first century promises even better, faster, and more secure communications capabilities, allowing information to be exchanged in the form of voice, text, images, and video. New systems will allow previously incompatible technologies to interoperate, that is, work together to provide seamless communication between different forces. The battlefield will continue to be a smoky, hazy, dusty, and noisy place, but increasingly less "foggy."

A LIFESAVER: THE JOINT
TACTICAL RADIO SYSTEM

The Joint Tactical Radio System (JTRS) is the army's major tele-communications upgrade project (see Fig. 3–1). JTRS will provide

JTRS Cluster 1 Airborne Radio

JTR S Cluster 1 Ground Radio

FIGURE 3–1.   JTRS SYSTEM COMPONENTS.

a family of software-programmable radios. JTRS aims to provide reliable multichannel voice, data, image, and video communications and to eliminate communications problems caused by aging and inadequate legacy systems.

JTRS is designed to be:

- Modular, enabling additional capabilities and features to be added to JTR sets.

- Scalable, enabling additional capacity (bandwidth and channels) to be added to JTR sets.

- Backwards compatible, allowing JTRS to communicate with the legacy radios it will eventually replace.

- Network capable, allowing dynamic intranetwork and internetwork routing for data transport that is transparent to the radio operator.

Current tactical communications systems evolved to meet service-specific and mission-specific requirements. This specialized functionality—their radio-specific design—has greatly limited the ability of one system to communicate with another. In today's defense environment, real-time information and effective communication among joint forces are critical.

In the short term, JTRS provides interoperability through its ability to communicate with current tactical communications systems. In the future, JTRS will provide integrated information sharing through new waveforms, which will support joint operations. This interoperability will help meet the demands of joint tactical, logistical, and medical activities that ensure combatant effectiveness and safety.

When fully implemented, JTRS will carry real-time information the "last tactical mile" to the soldier in the field. JTRS promises greater success and safety by providing rapid information streams from various sources. With effective implementation, engagements will be won more quickly, and lives will be saved.

COMMANDO COMMUNICATIONS: AD HOC WIRELESS NETWORKS

Electrical engineers at the University of California—San Diego are leading a six-university effort to enable troops to set up mobile communications networks on the battlefield. The goal is to provide troops with lightweight wireless equipment designed for use during commando raids and in other hostile and rapidly changing environments.

Ad hoc networks form when communications devices automatically find each other without the benefit of centralized network control systems. Deployment is vastly more complicated in fluid tactical situations in which special challenges emerge, and the price of dropped communications can mean loss of life and mission failure. Among the difficulties: Devices must stay in touch while moving around, maintain stealth, and avoid the enemy's attempts to jam or eavesdrop on communications. The network must sustain itself when communications devices go out of range or are damaged or destroyed.

Equipment that would be used in a tactical ad hoc network ranges from mobile radios mounted in backpacks, laptops, and handheld computers to antennas mounted on vehicles such as tanks and Humvees that come and go, and even airborne relays to route data to and from command-and-control bases and headquarters.

Although in and of themselves, these devices are not new, one target of innovation for the project is the network protocol suite, a reference to the many programs used to manage communications. These typically are grouped into discrete steps or layers, an arrangement that robs a network of its ability to adapt to changing conditions. One goal of the project is to set up a cross-layer algorithm that will enable the different layers to join together and make decisions, for example to decide to rotate an antenna in response to lagging signal strength, or to rapidly switch partners in response to movement.

The team will also explore the use of new antenna technology, coding, and error-correction systems. One focus will be multiple-input/multiple-output (MIMO) devices endowed with multiple antennas. This new technology shows great potential for enabling communications in less than optimal circumstances. For example, in a recent study by Brian Banister, one of Zeidler's graduate student researchers, a ten-fold boost in channel capacity (compared to a one-way channel, given the same signal-to-noise ratios on each channel) was achieved using an eight-fold asymmetric MIMO channel. MIMO devices format signals using space-time coding; therefore, when decoding messages the receiver analyzes positional differences between pieces of a signal and the timing of the signal's arrival. Besides boosting channel capacity, the technique also helps pick up signals that might otherwise be blocked by interference or terrain obstacles, such as buildings and hills.

"The technology could also be useful to firefighters, police, and other responders to emergencies such as fires, earthquakes, or terrorist attacks that have knocked out existing communications infrastructure," says James Zeidler, the project's principal investigator and a research scientist and senior lecturer in the Electrical and Computer Engineering Department of UCSD's Jacobs School of Engineering.

PACKET BLAST: AN ULTRA-FAST, SECURE RADIO SYSTEM

Bell Lab researchers are developing an ultra-high-capacity, highly secure communications system for DARPA. The system will be based on mobile-networked MIMO technology, which uses multiple antennas to send and receive wireless signals at ultra-high speeds.

Lucent Technologies, a subsidiary of Bell Labs, will use its MIMO technology, called BLAST (Bell Labs Layered Space Time), to develop the world's first tactical, continually moving, and self-forming MIMO mobile network. The system, called Packet BLAST, will be designed to provide immediate enhancements to the military's communications, including vastly expanded capacity; much higher data rate communications in non-line-of-sight environments such as urban areas and forested terrains; and improved stealth communications to avoid detection and jamming attempts by adversaries.

BLAST essentially exploits a theoretical concept that many researchers believed was impossible. In most wireless environments, radio signals don't travel directly from transmitter to receiver, but are randomly scattered in transit before they reach the receiver. Bell Labs' scientists theorized, and later proved, that it is possible to use signal scattering to enhance rather than degrade transmission accuracy. In addition, the researchers proved that it is possible to have several transmissions occupy the same frequency band, allowing the spectrum to be used very efficiently and with greater capacity than can be obtained using single channels. The use of multiple antennas increases the rate of transmission in proportion to the number of antennas used to transmit the signal without requiring increased power.

Packet BLAST will use advanced MIMO algorithms for high spectral efficiency, providing more network capacity. The system will also use MIMO ad hoc networking protocols, which enable the network to continually self-form as troops and vehicles move. A multifunction software-defined radio will eliminate the need for troops to carry multiple radios that require different protocols in order to communicate.

Lucent hopes to provide an initial MIMO-based mobile ad hoc network showing a 20 times increase in spectral efficiency. In fall 2004, Lucent deployed the network using twenty sport utility vehicles at the Naval Air Engineering Station in Lakehurst, New Jersey. The vehicles were equipped with mobile communications gear that incorporated the Packet BLAST solution. The Packet BLAST mobile radios were subjected to constantly changing urban and rural environments, as well as stress-inducing capacity demands.

Lucent researchers are currently analyzing data generated by the test. "Once we've proven Packet BLAST's abilities in the field, we hope to apply this work to other DoD programs, such as Joint Tactical Radio System and Future Combat Systems," says Mike

Geller, director of Bell Labs' Government Communications Laboratory.

I SPY: ULTRA-WIDEBAND SECURITY

A team of Virginia Tech researchers is attempting to push ultra-wideband (UWB) radio technology into its next phase—one in which military communications can completely elude detection by nearby enemy troops, and all manner of home electronic systems can be operated wirelessly.

Funded by a $750,000 grant from DARPA, Michael Buehrer, an assistant professor of electrical and computer engineering and principal investigator on the project, and colleagues William Davis, Ahmad Safaai-Jazi, and Dennis Sweeney in the mobile and portable radio research group at Virginia Tech are figuring out how UWB pulses are propagated and how those pulses can be recognized by potential receivers.

As Buehrer explains, UWB transmission—from a radar device, for example—uses ultra-short pulses that distribute power over a wide range of the radio frequency spectrum. Ideally, because the power density is dispersed across the spectrum, UWB transmissions won't interfere with the signals on narrow-band frequencies, such as AM or FM radio or cell phone signals. In fact, UWB transmissions pose so little threat of interference with licensed frequencies that the Federal Communications Commission (FCC) is now allowing companies to operate UWB technology within the 3- to 10-gigahertz range without radio spectrum licenses. "Ultrawideband technology offers unique advantages for communication compared to traditional narrow-band systems," says Buehrer.

The bandwidth of UWB signals is so wide that signal energy is available for use at both high and low frequencies. "The low-frequency content of UWB devices can penetrate solid structures, [and], the high-frequency content can detect the details of objects." These capabilities make UWB radar devices excellent surveillance tools.

As a result, UWB has the potential to bring about advances in communications technologies. Buehrer notes that "because of the low level of energy in UWB signals, a military unit using the technology could communicate without a nearby enemy even perceiving that transmissions are taking place."

In the first phase of the DARPA-sponsored project, Buehrer and his colleagues will develop models to show the characteristics of UWB transmitted pulses and how they will look to receivers. The research team hopes to continue the project into a second phase, using these models to design UWB receivers.

Buehrer believes that the FCC will continue to allow UWB devices to operate without licenses, which should help the technology proliferate outside the military. "UWB already has a long history," he notes. "The technology has been used in radar devices for some time. Actually, it's been around since Marconi transmitted the first telegraph signals."

MINISAR: RECONNAISSANCE AND WEAPON GUIDANCE SYSTEM

The National Nuclear Security Administration's Sandia National Laboratories is planning to fly the smallest synthetic aperture radar (SAR) ever used for reconnaissance on unmanned aerial vehicles (UAVs) nearing the size of model airplanes. Eventually this same technology will be used on precision-guided weapons and space applications.

Weighing less than 30 pounds, the miniSAR (Fig. 3–2) will be one-fourth the weight and one-tenth the volume of its predecessors, which currently fly on larger UAVs, such as the General Atomics' Predator. It is the latest design produced by Sandia, and the result of more than 20 years of related research and development.

The new miniSAR will have the same capabilities as its larger cousins: It will be able to take high-resolution (4-inch) images in any type of weather—at night, in dust storms, and so on. The only difference will be range. With its larger antenna and higher transmitter power, the larger SAR can produce an image in the 35 kilo-

FIGURE 3–2.   MINISAR TAKES FLIGHT.

meter range; the miniSAR is expected to achieve a range of about 15 kilometers—more than adequate for small UAV applications, such as surveillance. SARs are commonly used for military reconnaissance purposes.

MiniSAR is a revolutionary step forward and will open up a whole new class of applications, says George Sloan, Sandia project leader for miniSAR development. Sloan and fellow Sandia researchers Dale Dubbert and Armin Doerry created the current approach for miniaturized SARs years ago. New miniaturized components are now turning theory into reality. The effort incorporates a number of key technologies, including mechanical design, digital miniaturization, radio frequency (RF) miniaturization, and navigation expertise.

The new miniSAR consists of two major subsystems: (1) an Antenna Gimbal Assembly (AGA), the pointing system that consists of the antenna, mounting gimbal, and transmitter, and (2) the Radar Electronics Assembly (REA), the system's signal generator, receiver, and processors. The AGA beams and receives the radio frequency, and the REA is the electronics package that generates the radar signals, controls the system, processes the data, and transforms it into an image.

Through the creation of new ultra-lightweight antennas and miniaturization of the gimbal, the miniSAR team was able to reduce the AGA portion from 60 pounds, as in current UAV systems, to 18 pounds. Through novel adaptation of state-of-the-art digital and RF technologies, the REA was reduced from about 60 pounds to 8. Future versions of miniSAR will shrink the total weight to less than 10 pounds by leveraging both in-development and yet-to-be-developed Sandia microsystems technologies.

The miniSAR will have two primary applications. First, it will be used for reconnaissance on small UAVs, which can carry a payload of 50 pounds—considerably less than the weight of existing radars. Today, small UAVs are limited to carrying video or infrared cameras. A 30-pound miniSAR will allow small UAVs to carry additional sensors that together will provide a very detailed reconnaissance picture.

The second application is in precision-guided weapons. Current guidance systems for these weapons rely on target designation methods that are subject to jamming and have trouble operating in bad weather and dust storms. MinSAR is resistant to these problems. Previous SAR versions were too big, too heavy, and too expensive to use in precision-guidance applications.

Sloan notes that the researchers are now very close, perhaps within a couple of years, to having a miniSAR compatible with the small UAV requirements for cost, size, and weight. They are "a little further away" for precision-guided weapons, but are on the path to making it possible. Sloan says the miniSAR is near to being flight tested. The principal remaining tasks include the integration of the radar subsystems and the completion of the system software. Then the first version of miniSAR will be ready to go. Sloan anticipates that in 2005 the miniSAR will be flight tested on a Sandia test-bed aircraft. Then UAV vendors will demonstrate it on their own UAVs.

The transfer of the technology to industry will follow. But even as all this happens, the Sandia researchers will continue to make improvements and help miniSAR evolve into something even better and smaller. "We fully expect miniSAR to be the next big splash," Sloan says.

SEEING OVER THE HILL: THE RECONNAISSANCE ROUND

Soldiers in battle are always trying to discern what's in front of them. Both victory and survival can depend on it. Yet too often, buildings, hills, forests, and jungles get in the way. Now a Georgia Tech Research Institute (GTRI) project is developing a novel way for small ground units to see past obstacles. Called the "reconnaissance round," it would let soldiers use small artillery weapons almost like a periscope (Fig. 3–3). They would fire skyward a device that transmits images of nearby terrain back to a laptop computer, which is standard equipment now among infantry units.

The reconnaissance round is the idea of Charles M. Stancil, a senior research engineer at GTRI's Aerospace, Transportation, and Advanced Systems Laboratory. The need for a device like the reconnaissance round first occurred to Stancil, a retired army officer, when he was fighting in Vietnam. "I happened to be in a situation where I really, really needed to see what was on the other side of a hill," he recalls. "I made a promise to myself that if I ever had the opportunity to fix that, I would." As he puts it, "The typical situation an infantry unit encounters is a small number of hostile forces, [whose location they do] not know exactly. Soldiers will be able to fire the recon round and have photos relayed to them right over the battlefield, [which will give them] a vertical perspective [on] how the enemy is positioned."

Currently, a ground unit requiring aerial information has to go up the chain of command to request satellite images or aerial photos from an uninhabited aerial vehicle such as Global Hawk. The process is time consuming, and equipment is expensive, Stancil says. By contrast, the recon round promises to be quick, convenient, and relatively inexpensive at $1,200 per device.

FIGURE 3–3.   RECONNAISSANCE ROUND.

To minimize per-unit costs, the development team opted for a fixed-lens system, rather than a sophisticated zoom lens. Some sources quoted prices of $15,000-plus per lens, Stancil says, but his team found an existing lens system that cost only about $75. Black and white ground images seem to work as well as color, and may turn out to be more practical, too, because the smaller file size of such digital images enables faster transmission than larger color files.

Stancil emphasizes the system's simplicity, as well as its speed and relatively inexpensive price tag. Also, frontline troops can easily use the device under pressure. "We have put a great deal of effort into simplifying the interface," he says, "so that all you have to do is point and click, and then open it up and see the imagery."

The 2-pound, 6-inch-long reconnaissance device, made from off-the-shelf parts such as digital camera components, would be used in weapons like mortars that launch shells high in the air. Far above the battlefield, a separation charge opens a parachute, and the surveillance device floats down, transmitting digital images as it descends. "It can detect a human being from 1,800 feet in the air," Stancil says.

Typically deployed at a height of about 1,800 to 2,000 feet, the reconnaissance round has a field of view of 600 feet by 400 feet and can view terrain as far away as 3.1 miles (5,000 meters). The device sends back four to five digital photos before it hits the ground, after which it self-destructs to prevent its use by an enemy. Currently, no such shell-based reconnaissance devices exist in the military arsenal, Stancil notes.

The reconnaissance round is mechanically analogous to an illumination round, which typically is fired from a mortar and uses a flare suspended from a parachute to light up the area below. Although the recon round has good low-light performance, it could be used in conjunction with an illumination round in extreme low-light situations. Researchers are currently testing and validating the recon round, now entering its second year of development for the Office of Naval Research (ONR). A working prototype has been successfully test fired from an 81-millimeter mortar at a military range, and Stancil's team is fine-tuning the device using a compressed-gas-propelled launcher.

Stancil is waiting to have the recon round approved by the military for full-scale engineering development. A "go" decision would likely kick off recon-round development for three other compatible weapons—the 60-millimeter mortar, the 4.2-inch mortar, and the 40-millimeter grenade launcher.

For the numerous tests necessary to fine-tune the user interface, Stancil's team developed a special nitrogen-propelled launcher so it could test-fire the recon round many times. The team used Atlanta-area sod farms as a substitute for a government test range for the compressed-gas-launcher test. The sprawling sod farms have many attributes of a military test range, including a remote location and a dearth of trees and utility wires. "Using these farms has saved tremendous dollars and time," Stancil says. "If we had to go to a government range every time we wanted to test-fire, we wouldn't be anywhere near the point of achievement that we are now in the program."

SEARCH AND RESCUE: TINY RECONNAISSANCE ROBOTS

Imagine tiny robots snaking their way through collapsed buildings on search-and-rescue missions, receiving instructions and transmitting vital image data about the location of humans trapped in rubble. Amy Bell, an assistant professor of electrical and computer engineering at Virginia Tech, foresees just such a world.

Robots that use wireless communications devices to receive and transmit data already exist. "In fact," Bell notes, "Robin Murphy, a University of South Florida professor, used reconnaissance robots in confined, hazardous locations at the World Trade Center site after September 11 to transmit data to rescue workers."

However, size is a problem for mobile agents on reconnaissance missions because the transmission of images requires a hefty power source. "Small robots that can make their way into cramped spaces have to be tethered to power sources in order to receive and send data transmissions, and the tethers limit their range," she says. "Larger robots can carry their own battery packs, but they can't maneuver in small spaces."

An expert in signal processing, Bell began working on ways to compress images in 1999. "For example, downloading an Internet site that contains several photographs can take a good deal of time," she explains. "But suppose, instead of sending the graphics in their original form—let's say 300 megabytes that might take 10 minutes to download—we could compress those images into 10 megabytes that would download in only one-third of a minute and the compressed images would look the same as the originals."

Bell's goal is to compress images in ways that will significantly reduce the power required for small, mobile agents to transmit images in wireless networks. She is working on the project with Joan Carletta, an electrical engineering professor at the University of Akron whose specialty is computer hardware. "We've already developed a novel idea that represents a first step toward implementing our goal," Bell says. "It's a method of transforming images in hardware that loses very little of the data's original quality." Bell will develop algorithms, or mathematical procedures, for perfecting the data image compression, and Carletta will devise a method for making those algorithms work in hardware.

If they succeed, data transmission power requirements could be reduced so that small robots outfitted with small batteries would be able to move freely where no human can—or should—go. In fact, the success of Bell's and Carletta's project could result in technology advances beyond the use of diminutive robots for search and rescue. For example, soldiers who need to transmit and receive data during field operations could be relieved of the burden of heavy battery packs. Another potential use of the technology would be equipping "micro-air" vehicles—small reconnaissance aircraft—with image transmission devices. Bell and Carletta are continuing their research under a National Science Foundation grant.

CSIRO MANTIS: AN INTELLIGENT HELICOPTER

Australian scientists have developed a "brain" that makes practicable the production of a low-cost, intelligent, small helicopter, which will perform many difficult and dangerous tasks heretofore undertaken only by human fliers. In effect, the CSIRO Mantis can simply be told where to go and what to do, and it will go off, do the job, and find its own way home, unassisted.

The CSIRO Mantis, a vertical-takeoff unmanned aerial vehicle (UAV), offers a host of new ways of doing things. For example, because there is no risk of life, the CSIRO Mantis can get a close-up look at high-rise building facades and windows or fly under bridges, and structural and geological overhangs for a "look up" view. "Mantis makes it possible for fleets of small drone helicopters to do jobs now done by conventional aircraft," says Peter Corke, principal research scientist at CSIRO Complex Systems Integration. "This could lead to a quantum leap in the speed of air–sea rescue efforts, [giving searchers the ability to cover] many square kilometers faster [with] many small aircraft searching at the same time," he notes.

Besides rescue missions, CSIRO Mantis's greatest potential military application lies in surveillance, particularly in tight, closed-in places, such as mountainous regions and cities. It can also be used as a stationary observation post, focusing on a single location without having to circle like an unmanned airplane. The vehicle's vertical-takeoff capability means that it can be launched and retrieved in places where open space is limited, such as downtown areas.

"The CSIRO Mantis [has overcome] many machine intelligence and cost issues, which have prevented the development of small, almost disposable unmanned air vehicles," says Corke. "It was also our aim to develop an inexpensive system where the cost of the electronics, now almost 10 times more expensive than the helicopter, would instead be about the same price."

The major task in developing Mantis, says Corke, was to produce an inertial sensing system to control and provide flight stability and a computer vision system to guide the aircraft. "The inertial sensing system behaves some[thing] like our inner ear, providing balance and indicating the orientation of the helicopter in the air." The instrument, custom developed by CSIRO, uses low-cost MEMS (micro-electromechanical system) sensors; it is fabricated from magnesium alloy and weighs only 75 grams. "This is much lighter than current technology and is one of the major reasons we were able to make the brains of the Mantis light enough to be carried by such a small helicopter," says Corke.

The vision system uses two miniature cameras and powerful CSIRO-developed software running on a medium-powered onboard computer. "Just as we use our two eyes to estimate the distance of an object, the helicopter uses the data from the two cameras to estimate its height above ground, a very important thing to know," says Corke. "The computer also observes the changes in the image over time and from this it estimates its speed over the ground."

Developing lightweight components and dealing with vibration has been an important factor in the success of the Mantis. The Mantis itself is a little over 0.5 meters high and just short of 1.5 meters long, with a custom-built aluminum frame and landing gear.

The military is also interested in UAVs, notes Corke. "They have generally used very precise GPS guidance equipment, which requires an expensive unit onboard the aircraft as well as expensive equipment on the ground," he says. "While GPS may seem like an ideal technique [for this purpose], it has many drawbacks in practice, particularly in [heavily developed areas] near large structures, which can obscure or reflect the signals from the GPS satellites."

THE RAVEN: THE SOLDIER'S EYES

Ground troops in company-size or smaller units are getting new help from above with an emerging class of UAVs compact enough to be carried in rucksacks. The stealthy Raven, developed by the U.S. Army Soldier Systems Center in Natick, Massachusetts, U.S.

Special Operations Command (USSOCOM) Special Operations Acquisition Logistics-Technology, and AeroVironment in Monrovia, California, is among the latest in small UAVs that give soldiers a bird's-eye view of the battlefield for beyond line-of-sight reconnaissance and surveillance.

The Raven resulted from the army's Military Operations in Urban Terrain Advanced Concept Technology Demonstration (MOUT ACTD) intelligence gathering and dissemination requirements, which sought to improve the operational effectiveness of soldiers and marines in urban and other built-up areas by integrating advanced technologies and associated tactics, techniques, and procedures.

With the completion of MOUT ACTD in 2002, the ACTD and Urban Technology office at Natick transitioned to the USSOCOM-sponsored Pathfinder ACTD, an effort to integrate unattended ground vehicles, UAVs, and smart sensors into a mobile, self-forming network providing enhanced situational awareness, command, control, and communications to commanders and assault forces for urban reconnaissance.

Raven, introduced in 2004, has its roots in the Pointer UAV and derives from both the MOUT and Pathfinder ACTDs. "Up until [MOUT ACTD], UAVs were used as a strategic asset at higher echelons," says Andy Mawn, ACTD and Urban Technology program manager. "The breakthroughs [came when] we could make them for light infantrymen and the technology to operate it in that size [became viable]. . . . We understand soldiers at the dismounted infantry level," Mawn adds, explaining how his office became involved with aircraft. "From MOUT ACTD, we had constant interaction with soldiers. They're the real designers. We always kept it focused on small and simple."

The Raven adopts the same basic design and function of the Pointer but in the smaller package soldiers need—the aircraft's wingspan shrunk from 9 to 4.5 feet and its weight went from 9 to 4 pounds. The device is designed for two operators, a pilot and mission controller, although it can work with only one, and is deployed with four to six troops who can share the equipment load and secure the perimeter, according to Mawn. Other components in a Raven package are the ground control unit, video display terminal or laptop monitor, and batteries, which total about 30 pounds.

"They're learning it's worth the extra weight. You know they like it when they're willing to carry it without being ordered [to]," says Susan McKinney, deputy program manager. The aircraft is assembled in less than 3 minutes using plastic clips to fasten together seven gray modular Kevlar composite pieces, which are stored in two cases. Depending on the mission, the aircraft's detachable nose carries a daytime video camera capable of simultaneous front and side views, and an infrared video camera with front view or side view.

Hand launched from a standing position (similar to passing a football), the aircraft gains altitude quickly and is directed by an operator-controller when it is in full manual mode, steered left or right at a constant altitude in the semi-autonomous mode, or completely self-controlled in the autonomous mode.

Powered by a single propeller connected to a direct-drive electric engine, the aircraft's advanced avionics steady the flight while a GPS and electronic compass provide redundant navigation systems in case one fails. The ground control unit guides the aircraft, programs mission waypoints, and displays what is seen by the aircraft.

From as far as 6 miles away, the system transmits live airborne video images and location information to the ground control unit and remote video terminal, and records the video for later analysis. Troops can track the enemy, secure convoys, protect base camps, identify targets, and assess battle damage.

"A lead vehicle in a convoy can fly the Raven and see what's up ahead. It helps air force tactical air controllers describe the target from a pilot's perspective," Mawn says. "They're still figuring out uses for it. Flying it is simple, but what to do with the information is the challenge."

In the event the radio signal is lost, the aircraft goes into "fly home" or "rally point" mode so that it can be safely recovered. Flight time is limited to about 90 minutes, and landing is nothing less than an operator-controlled crash, the pieces scattering apart as it is commanded into a "deep stall." Underbelly padding helps dissipate energy, but it's subject to damage if it strikes a pointed surface, such as jagged rock.

More than a hundred of the Raven systems went into production in 2004, with deployment to support troops in Afghanistan and Iraq, according to Mawn. Training is ongoing for units planning on flying the Raven. Military officials will not reveal the total number of UAVs being used in Afghanistan or Iraq, citing operational security. "Demand has been so high for the system, we would have [preferred to experiment] with them more, but we haven't had the chance to quantify system performance or work with the TTPs (tactics, techniques, and procedures)," Mawn says.

Planned upgrades include an even smaller and lighter ground control unit, a higher resolution video screen, enhanced infrared video camera resolution, simultaneous front and side infrared camera capability, and an antenna that reduces potential exposure to the enemy.

BIRD'S-EYE VIEW: A ROBOT THAT CAN FLY

Sunil K. Agrawal, a University of Delaware professor of mechanical engineering, is working on the design and construction of small robotic devices that mimic the flight of birds and insects—in particular, the hummingbird and the hawkmoth (Fig. 3–4). Agrawal anticipates that once fully developed, the devices, flying in flock-like formations, will be able to carry miniature cameras and transmit surveillance data back to a central computer for processing.

The idea for robotic birds came to Agrawal in 2002, and he found support for his project from U.S. Air Force officials at Eglin Air Force Base in Valparaiso, Florida. The military uses were readily apparent: If the robotic birds can provide a stable platform for cameras, they can create detailed maps of nearly any environment. Industrial uses are also possible; for example, the birds can compile important information on large factory floors. Additionally, there are police and rescue applications, such as SWAT teams, able

FIGURE 3–4.   HOLDING TINY ROBOT BIRD.

to gather valuable data by sending the birds in to map the interiors of collapsed buildings.

Agrawal's laboratory receives funding from the National Science Foundation, the U.S. Air Force, the National Institute of Standards and Technology, and the National Institutes of Health.

While the need for such devices in surveillance and telemetry has existed for some time, the technology permitting such miniaturization is relatively new and still evolving. "We are quite enthusiastic about being able to build these machines," says Agrawal, whose research team is focused on the design, fabrication, and control of a variety of robotic devices in addition to the birds.

Early versions of the robotic birds were made of balsa wood and powered by rubber band engines that made the wings flap. When a subsequent design, with battery-powered wings, took flight, they noticed that "When it flew, birds from nearby came and circled around it," which was totally unexpected according to

Agrawal. That robotic bird spent 2 minutes in flight, but was not equipped for remote control.

Current designs have replaced the balsa components with carbon fiber composites, and paper wings with Mylar film (a cellophane-like material), dropping the total weight from 50 to 15 grams and strengthening the frame to withstand crashes. The research team is now working to optimize the design so that the mass and power can be kept to a minimum. Agrawal hopes to further miniaturize the birds to the point in which they are small enough to fit in the palm of a hand. At the same time, they are working to integrate controls to guide the robot's flight.

To control a group of birds in flight, Agrawal will turn to technologies he has developed to make land-bound robots work in unison. "We want to demonstrate that the flapping wing machines can be built and optimized and, eventually, we would like to expand from a single flying machine to a group of cooperative flying machines," Agrawal says. "This will be in the future . . . but it is where I think we would like to go."

For now, Agrawal's goal is to build a better bird. The research team is studying individual wing motions, and looking at birds and insects to better understand how they get lift. The hummingbird is a valuable model because it can hover, an ability that is key to effective surveillance. "Making things mimic nature is much more difficult than it might seem," Agrawal points out. "It is scientifically fascinating, but also extremely challenging." The research team plans to take new designs to a wind tunnel, where the birds will be tested in various flying attitudes to gather data on force and torque. That information will be used to determine how to improve and control the movement of the birds, and future designs will then be refined using computer models.

"CAN YOU HEAR ME?": ROBOTIC VOICE NAVIGATION

Another innovative approach to robot control—still in its testing phase—is being investigated at the University of Toronto. UT researchers have created a robot that features a motorized base and elevated speakers that play prerecorded phrases. The sounds are picked up by an array of microphones placed in the environment that locate the robot on a master computer's virtual map. The computer then tells the robot where to move. If the robot encounters an object in its path using its hair-thin "whiskers," it backs up, reorients itself, then plots a new course around the obstacle.

The robot's prototype application is as a museum tour guide. Today, museum guides carry a clipboard and wave a flag to help straggling tourists find the group. In the future, talking robotic guides carrying a customized microchip and four-way speakers could lead tourists from exhibit to exhibit. "This is a very unique solution to navigating," says Parham Aarabi, a professor in UT's Edward S. Rogers Sr. Department of Electrical and Computer Engineering and the project's lead researcher. "Using an array of stationary microphones in the museum, this kind of system could accurately help the robot find its location using the sounds that it generates," says Aarabi.

Beyond museums, the technology has numerous military and homeland security applications. The robot could, for example, be deployed in hazardous environments like collapsed structures or chemically contaminated buildings. It could also be used to quickly guide troops through complex and confusing terrains.

DRAGON RUNNER: A REMOTE-CONTROLLED "THROWABLE" ROBOT

Carnegie Mellon University robotics researchers, in conjunction with the U.S. Marine Corps' Warfighting Laboratory, have developed a small, throwable, remote-controlled prototype robot designed for surveillance in urban settings. The robot, known as Dragon Runner, is able to see around corners and deliver information to marines, which keeps them out of danger in urban settings where human access is impractical, dangerous, or unsustainable. The Dragon Runner project is managed and funded by the Warfighting Laboratory, which is part of the Marine Corps Combat

Development Command. The system has been under development for more than 2 years and has already undergone rigorous testing in a variety of austere environments.

"The Dragon Runner can function in loose soil with small obstacles but is most effective on relatively flat surfaces like streets and sidewalks, making it ideal for an urban, desert environment," says Captain Dave Moreau, Dragon Runner project officer with the Marine Corps Warfighting Lab. "We have conducted a thorough evaluation of its capabilities in an urban, desert environment at both the former George Air Force Base, in Victorville, California, and Southwest Research Institute in San Antonio, Texas. The next step is to test Dragon Runner operationally in theater."

The architect behind Dragon Runner is Hagen Schempf, a principal research scientist in Carnegie Mellon's Robotics Institute. During his career, Schempf has designed robotic systems for asbestos removal, nuclear waste remediation, and cleanup of underground storage tanks containing toxic materials. "Dragon Runner is the lightest, smallest, most rugged, readily portable robot system for remote scouting operations in existence today," he says. "It has the potential to be the eyes and ears of the marines in forward urban operations, allowing them to gather intelligence without being in harm's way. It is a tool that reduces potential lethal exposure to our troops by decreasing the amount of time that they expose themselves to danger."

The Warfighting Laboratory describes Dragon Runner as a small, four-wheeled, all-wheel-drive, invertible, tossable, remotely operated, low-cost, man-portable, mobile ground sensor designed to increase situational awareness at the small unit level (i.e., company and below) in urban environments. In today's modern battle spaces, potential enemies capitalize on the asymmetric nature of urban areas. In response, Dragon Runner can provide real-time imagery of tactical objectives and potential dangers beyond a marine's line of sight during day or night. Dragon Runner's non-active and invertible suspension allows it to be tossed upstairs, over a wall, or through a window at any time—day or night—for easy, rapid deployment.

Dragon Runner can stand in sentry mode by using several

onboard motion and audio sensors to monitor selected areas. It may also be configured to carry mission-specific payloads. The complete system includes the vehicle, an operator control system, and a controller configured for one-handed operation, all held in a custom backpack. Dragon Runner has a top speed of more than 20 miles per hour but also can be operated with slow, deliberate control. It operates in a mode similar to modern video games and can be deployed from its backpack in less than 3 seconds.

In addition to his work at the Robotics Institute, Schempf is chief scientist at Automatika, a Pittsburgh-based company he founded in 1995 that develops novel, high-value-added robotic and automation systems. Automatika was responsible for the development of Dragon Runner's rugged distributed vehicle electronics and the development of its impact-tolerant chassis and shell.

Automatika has licensed the Dragon Runner technology from Carnegie Mellon, which is exploring the civilian opportunities for this system for such things as civil defense, SWAT, patrolling the nation's borders, and in criminal defense.

X MARKS THE SPOT: LAND MINE–SNIFFING ROBOT

Four Johns Hopkins University undergraduate engineering students have designed and built a remote-controlled robotic vehicle to find deadly land mines in rugged terrain and mark their location with a spray of paint. The prototype has been given to professional explosive detection researchers as a model for a low-cost robot that humanitarian groups and military troops could use to prevent mine-related deaths and injuries.

The project resulted from a challenge to the students by Carl V. Nelson, a principal staff physicist at The Johns Hopkins University Applied Physics Laboratory. He presented his requirements last fall to a team of students enrolled in the two-semester Engineering Design Project course offered by the Department of Mechanical Engineering at Johns Hopkins. "I asked the students to develop a vehicle that could get off the road, off the clear paths, and go into rougher terrain like bushes and high grass, where mine detection would be difficult to do by hand," Nelson says.

The need for such a device was clear. Nelson pointed to a United Nations estimate that more than 100 million land mines are deployed in 70 countries worldwide, planted during military conflicts dating back as far as World War II. The cheap but highly dangerous devices can be set off by civilians as well as soldiers, and more than 2,000 people are killed or maimed by mine explosions each month, the United Nations estimates. Nelson is one of many researchers looking for safe, efficient, and relatively inexpensive ways to locate the hazards.

To carry Nelson's sensors through rough terrain, the Johns Hopkins undergraduates designed a two-piece vehicle that rolls on tank-type treads. The front portion moves the robot, using two cordless-power drill motors connected to a sealed lead-acid battery. Atop the drive segment is a color video camera, enabling a human operator to see what the robot encounters. The drive segment is attached to a second unit that houses a simple metal-detection coil obtained from an off-the-shelf treasure-hunting device. (This metal detector will be replaced by more sophisticated sensors if the model is utilized by funded researchers.) The rear segment also is equipped with a small storage tank and a spray paint nozzle to mark the spot where a possible mine is located. The vehicle can spray about 40 times before the paint tank must be recharged.

To guide the robot from a safe distance, the students constructed a battery-powered controller with a joystick to steer the vehicle. The controller also features a small video screen displaying real-time images from the robot's camera. When metal is detected, a "beep" is heard over a speaker on the controller or through headphones worn by the operator. A switch on the controller then activates the paint sprayer to mark the spot. The robot's camera transmits video up to about 100 feet from the controller; the vehicle's movement can be controlled from a distance of about 500 feet.

The robotic vehicle was built largely with plastic and other nonmetal parts to reduce cost and weight, and perhaps more important the use of nonmetal parts avoids triggering false positive readings. The two-segment design also spreads out the robot's weight, making the device less likely to set off a mine.

The four undergraduate inventors—Edoardo Biancheri, 22, of Rio De Janeiro, Brazil; Dan Hake, 21, from Wilton, Connecticut; Dat Truong, 22, from Methuen, Massachusetts; and Landon Unninayar, 22, from Columbia, Maryland—were all seniors. Hake, Truong, and Unninayar majored in mechanical engineering, and graduated from Johns Hopkins in May 2004. Biancheri completed his undergraduate studies in December 2004 with a double major in mechanical engineering and economics.

Working within a sponsored budget of $8,000, the students spent about $5,000 to design and build their prototype. They estimate the vehicle could be mass-produced for $1,000 or less, not including the cost of more sophisticated detection sensors. Nelson plans to show the prototype to his U.S. Army funding sponsors as an example of the type of low-cost mine detection robot that could help prevent death and injury worldwide. "I think the students did an excellent job," Nelson says. "They met just about all the requirements that I set out for them."

The land mine detection robot was one of nine Johns Hopkins projects completed this year by undergraduates in the engineering design course. The class is taught by Andrew F. Conn, a Johns Hopkins graduate with more than 30 years of experience in public and private research and development. Each team of three or four students, working within budgets of up to $10,000, had to design a device, purchase or fabricate the parts, and assemble the final product. Corporations, government agencies, and nonprofit groups provided the assignments and funding.

STRETCH: E-TEXTILES FOR BATTLEFIELD SOUND DETECTION

For decades, electronics have been getting smaller and smaller. Now engineers are turning to one of humankind's oldest arts—

weaving—for a cost-effective way of making certain devices bigger and bigger.

The STRETCH (named for this textile's flexibility) program is a cooperative venture between the University of Southern California and Virginia Tech that is now testing a prototype e-textile—a special cloth interwoven with microelectronic components. Modern methods of detection use arrays of individual detectors, arranged in a pattern, and combine the reports from all into a detailed image using sophisticated computational algorithms. The cloth functions as a supersensitive detection array to pinpoint sources of faint sounds, specifically the sounds of distant vehicles moving on future battlefields. According to its creators, this is the first time an e-textile has been produced that can perform all aspects of this complicated process.

"Modern methods of making fabrics allow extraordinary control over materials and properties," says Robert Parker, director of the Arlington, Virginia, campus of the USC School of Engineering's Information Sciences Institute, and coprincipal investigator on STRETCH. "And cloth has properties that can be very useful for certain electronic applications. We can easily and cheaply make very large pieces of cloth, light and very strong, that can be stretched over frames into any desired shape."

The material Parker and his coinvestigator, Mark Jones of the Configurable Computing Laboratory at Virginia Polytechnic Institute and State University, have created could be deployed in various ways: as a parachute, a tent, a camouflage net, a sail, or simply as a bolt of cloth that can be rolled compactly away until needed. A tent constructed out of the fabric, for example, could automatically alert its occupants to approaching vehicles. Other types of electronics woven into fabrics could help users manage environmental settings, provide control capabilities, or pick up radio signals. However deployed, the idea is the same, according to the researchers.

Parker and his ISI colleagues have long been working on arrays made up of small, stand-alone detectors that are individually placed in the environment, and communicate with each other by radio. But embedding similar units into fabric has advantages, according to Parker. "The signals they exchange can be carried on wires in the fabric. This greatly lowers the power requirements to operate the system." Additionally, signal exchanges by radio can potentially be picked up by an adversary, giving away not only the fact that surveillance is underway, but also the position of those doing the surveillance—a potentially fatal drawback in modern battlefield conditions.

"Forming [the detection system] into a fabric makes it electronically silent," says Jones. Additionally, while embedding the detectors in fabric sacrifices the flexibility of individual stand-alone units, it ensures the units will automatically be in the right positions relative to each other to do their jobs optimally.

Many problems still have to be resolved before the technology can reach the field. "While fabric-manufacturing technology is advanced, we expect that the large number of components and the inherent imprecision in the process will make it difficult to weave very large, fault-free arrays," Parker notes. Making the material tough enough to stand up to weather and rough handling in field conditions is another challenge. However, in preliminary tests, the material has proven robust. It can be rolled (though not folded) and unrolled, without damage. And even when a substantial number of the individual units fail, the detector is still able to function effectively.

Will soldiers' wardrobes someday include sound detector sweaters, satellite signal antenna hats, or chemical sniffer vests? Not right away, but perhaps soon.

GOOD VIBRATIONS: COMMUNICATING WITHOUT SIGHT OR SOUND

University of Central Florida researchers are testing whether the military could alert soldiers to battlefield threats through vibrations and, therefore, rely less on other, more distracting forms of communications, such as verbal messages and visual displays mounted in their helmets.

Communicating with soldiers presents many challenges for the military. Soldiers must clearly understand information about threats, because miscommunications can leave them vulnerable to attacks and wrong responses can be deadly. Richard Gilson, a psychology professor who is the lead researcher on the project, believes the military can best convey information without lights and sounds that could alert the enemy to soldiers' locations. According to Gilson, helmet-mounted displays block some soldiers' views of their surroundings, and soldiers can be so overwhelmed with visual and auditory information that they aren't paying enough attention to the sights and sounds around them.

Gilson and the UCF researchers are evaluating ways to send coded signals through miniature devices that vibrate. "Clearly," Gilson says, "there's a concern for our soldiers, allied soldiers, and civilians [and] we want to find out if there's a better way to convey information about threats. I seriously think we can save some lives with this."

Initial research will test how well UCF students understand information relayed through vibrating sensors on their bodies compared with information they hear through speakers in the room. The UCF researchers will focus on whether coded vibrations are a more effective way to relay information, rather than on specific details such as what type of device should be used to send them or where the sensors should be placed on the soldiers' bodies. If the research shows communication through vibrations to be more effective, then the military would investigate how to best put it into practice. It's possible that the vibrations could be relayed through devices built into belts, inside helmets, or even in mouthpieces, says Gilson. The new system could be used along with the current methods of communication.

Future phases of the research promise to get more specific, as the researchers would then try to find out how much detail they could communicate through patterns of vibrations.

BURIED DANGER: SEISMIC LAND MINE DETECTION SYSTEM

Millions of land mines are buried worldwide, and such weapons were responsible for an estimated 16,000 injuries and deaths in 2002 (most recent data available).

Georgia Institute of Technology researchers are making progress with a land mine detection system that could ultimately help prevent such losses. The system uses high-frequency seismic waves to slightly displace (less than one–ten-thousandth of an inch) both soil and objects contained within the soil. A noncontacting radar sensor then measures the results, creating a visual representation of the displacement that reveals the buried mines.

This seismic-wave system offers potential advantages over existing electromagnetic-wave techniques used in metal detectors and ground-penetrating radar (GPR). Metal detectors and GPRs can locate mines successfully, but they have difficulty locating the small, plastic antipersonnel mines that have become increasingly prevalent. Metal detectors and GPRs can also be confused by ground clutter—rocks, sticks, or scraps of metal—resulting in false alarms.

Laboratory and limited field tests have demonstrated that because plastic mines have very different mechanical properties from soil and ground clutter seismic waves are able to detect and distinguish them from common ground clutter. "When a wave hits a land mine, resonance builds over the top of the mine, triggering a vibration that is bigger than the wave that excited it—and the vibration persists longer," says Waymond R. Scott Jr., a professor in Georgia Tech's School of Electrical and Computer Engineering (ECE) and principal investigator on the project.

Sponsored by the ONR, the U.S. Army Research Office, and the U.S. Army Night Vision & Electronic Sensors Systems Directorate, the mine detection project involves a multidisciplinary team of researchers at Georgia Tech, who started on this project in 1997 with computer modeling and lab experiments. Field testing began in fall 2001, and the researchers have conducted tests at seven sites so far. "Our results . . . were comparable to what we saw in the lab, which was very significant. That was a big hurdle for us," Scott says.

COSMIC NETWORK: GLOBAL WEATHER REPORT

Over the centuries, weather has played as much of a role in battle as many of the most powerful tactical weapons. Soon a revolutionary globe-spanning satellite network will furnish military leaders with round-the-clock weather data by intercepting signals from global positioning system (GPS) satellites. Using atmosphere-induced changes in the GPS radio signals, scientists will infer the state of the atmosphere above some 3,000 locations every 24 hours and over vast stretches of ocean inadequately profiled by current satellites and other tools. The $100 million mission is set to begin operation in 2005.

A U.S.–Taiwan partnership is developing the satellite network, called the Constellation Observing System for Meteorology, Ionosphere and Climate (COSMIC). The network is based on a system design provided by the University Corporation for Atmospheric Research (UCAR) in Boulder, Colorado. Taiwan's National Science Council and National Space Program Office (NSPO) and the U.S. National Science Foundation (NSF) are providing management and support for COSMIC. Additional support is being provided by NASA, NOAA, and the Department of Defense.

"The increased coverage will improve weather forecasts by providing data where there previously was none or not enough," says Ying-Hwa Kuo, project director for COSMIC (called ROC-SAT-3 in Taiwan). With six satellite receivers, COSMIC will collect a global, 3D data set expected to improve analyses of both weather and climate change. The system can help the navy guide its ships around potentially dangerous seas and give military planners better information about when to launch strategic ground operations. The technology also has multiple civilian applications. For example, by tracking temperature in the upper atmosphere (up to 30 miles high), COSMIC could help scientists determine if regions are cooling due to heat-trapping greenhouse gases closer to the earth's surface. COSMIC will also measure high-altitude electron density, potentially enhancing forecasts of ionospheric activity and "space weather." By taking measurements below 12 miles high, COSMIC could provide critical information on atmospheric water vapor, crucial for accurately predicting weather systems with precipitation.

COSMIC's satellites will probe the atmosphere using a technique known as radio occultation, which was developed in the

1960s to study other planets but more recently has been applied to the earth's atmosphere. Each satellite will intercept a GPS signal after it passes through (is occulted by) the atmosphere close to the horizon. Such a path brings the signal through a deep cross-section of the atmosphere. Variations in electron density, air density, temperature, and moisture bend the signal and change its speed. By measuring these shifts in the signal, scientists can determine the atmospheric conditions that produced them. The result: profiles along thousands of angled, pencil-like segments of atmosphere, each about 200 miles long and a few hundred feet wide.

Rather than replacing other observing systems, COSMIC will blend with them, filling in major gaps and enhancing computer forecast models. Many satellite-based products are like topographic maps that trace the contours of atmospheric elements. COSMIC is more akin to a set of probes that drill vertically through the depth of atmosphere. Thus, says Kuo, "COSMIC will complement the existing and planned U.S. meteorological satellites."

Radiosondes (weather sensors launched by balloon) have obtained vertical profiles since the 1930s. However, they are launched only twice a day in most spots, and few are deployed over the ocean. In contrast, the COSMIC data will be collected continuously across the globe. The GPS radio signals can be picked up by the low-orbiting COSMIC receivers even through clouds, which are an obstacle for satellite-borne instruments that sense infrared rays of the spectrum.

WIISARD: MASS CASUALTY TREATMENT

The use of sophisticated wireless technology to coordinate and enhance care of mass casualties that are the result of a military operation, terrorist attack, or natural disaster is the focus of a research project at the University of California—San Diego (UCSD).

The goal of the Wireless Internet Information System for Medical Response in Disasters (WIISARD) is to: (1) provide emergency personnel and disaster command centers with medical data to track and monitor the condition of hundreds to thousands of victims on a moment-to-moment basis, over a period of hours or days at the disaster site, (2) develop technologies to enhance communication among emergency team members, and (3) ensure their safety by tracking the "hot zone," or location and wind drift of any chemical or radioactive matter used as a weapon against civilians.

The WIISARD project director is Leslie Lenert, a UCSD associate professor of medicine and chief of the Laboratory for the Study of Patients' Preferences at the VA San Diego Healthcare System. Lenert, a physician, also holds an MS in Medical Information Sciences from Stanford University.

"We believe that the current technologies supporting acute field care of victims of disasters are simply inadequate," Lenert says. "The new technologies deployed by WIISARD will bring cutting-edge wireless Internet technologies from the hospital to the mass casualty field treatment station. Essentially, WIISARD is designed to overcome significant problems experienced in recent terrorist attacks." WIISARD also promises to revolutionize the treatment of wounded, injured, or sick troops. Essentially, the technology will allow field medics to instantly tap the expertise of the military's best medical experts whenever such consultation is necessary.

To develop a WIISARD prototype and test it in simulated disaster drills, the UCSD/VA team will partner with researchers from the California Institute for Telecommunications and Information Technology [Cal-(IT)²], its members in industry (including QUALCOMM, Verizon Wireless, Ericsson, and PhilMetric), the military (including the U.S. Navy's Space and Naval Warfare Systems Command), and faculty from the UCSD Jacobs School of Engineering and the San Diego Supercomputer Center. An important component of the project is participation by the San Diego Metropolitan Medical Strike Team (MMST), one of the first such teams established nationwide in 1996. The MMST is composed of firefighters, police, FBI, hazmat teams, paramedics, San Diego City Emergency Medical Services, and San Diego County public health and hospital representatives, among others.

Under current disaster plans, initial responders provide an

immediate scene assessment, followed by the establishment of a disaster command center. At the disaster scene, field providers evaluate patients, provide treatment, and prioritize individuals for transport to medical facilities. In the event of mass casualties, however, emergency personnel could be overwhelmed with thousands of victims in an environment contaminated with hazardous materials—a setting potentially fraught with inaccurate information, hampered communications, and limited resources.

Rather than attempting to create new software systems and devices to meet the needs of mass casualty care, WIISARD will customize existing software and hardware, and integrate existing systems. The result will be a first-of-its-kind wireless medical-response system for mass casualties. WIISARD will utilize radio frequency (RF) tags placed on all patients to track the location of victims and healthcare providers. The most severely ill patients will also receive a medical sensor, a fingertip pulse oximeter, which monitors the degree of blood oxygen saturation and pulse rate. Data from the RF tags and sensors will be sent to a collector unit that buffers, compresses, and wirelessly forwards data to a central database. These devices will provide field providers and the disaster command center with information on the location of each victim and his or her condition to aid in coordination of available resources.

The project will also equip frontline emergency responders with handheld devices called personal digital assistants (PDAs), which will provide location-based access to patient medical data and enhanced communications via instant messaging with field healthcare providers and the disaster command center. The system will monitor the location of toxic plumes from chemical or nuclear attacks, via a component of the PDA that displays a map of the immediate region, so that providers can avoid entering a hot zone while caring for patients. This technology is based on the use of sensors monitoring local weather conditions and advanced mathematical models to predict the weapons' effects.

WIISARD will maintain a record of medical care with a disaster database that's based on an electronic medical record system designed by UCSD emergency physician James Killeen and nurse

Donna Kelly. The system will also transmit medical data from the field to hospitals in a secure manner, and provide a record of patient transfer to specific hospitals.

WIISARD's multiple components will address various needs identified in the analysis of recent disaster response scenarios. During the September 11 attack, for example, communication between scene coordinators and hospitals was almost nonexistent. As a result, many victims were transported to inappropriate hospitals that lacked both critical facilities and staff. In addition, health-care providers and firefighters had difficulty communicating with one another. To resolve this problem, WIISARD will utilize hand-held PDAs based on wireless devices currently used by students at UCSD's Sixth College.

WIISARD's medical sensors will provide real-time data to field personnel and the command center to help avoid one of the tragedies of the 2002 terrorist attack in a Moscow theater where medical personnel later reported that most deaths resulted from lack of vital signs monitoring at the scene and an inability to organize care to determine who was breathing and who wasn't.

WIISARD's PDAs will have an Active First Responder (AFR) system designed to provide situational awareness to providers and the command center, so that responders don't accidentally move into hot zones. Initially, hot zones will be manually designated by the incident commander. As more data become available, computer models of weather and weapons' effects will be used to predict hot zones. The patient-location devices will also be able to alert the command center if patients attempt to leave the area, which could contaminate others. "Where technology can make a big difference is in awareness of danger zones for emergency first-responders and patients," says Theodore Chan, MMST's medical director. "For example, we saw in 9/11 that the scene commanders didn't know where providers were in the World Trade towers. They couldn't communicate to those in the second tower that the first tower had collapsed."

Field tests at government facilities give the researchers greater credibility because conditions are more realistic, and they can compare results to data from other research teams. What's more, the mines at government test sites have been buried for several years, which makes their detection more complicated. "It's much easier to detect a mine that's been buried recently because you've disturbed the soil," says George McCall, a senior research engineer in the Georgia Tech Research Institute's Electro-Optics, Environment and Materials Laboratory. "After a land mine has been in the ground for a while, the soil becomes weathered and more compact. This makes it harder to find, so it's a better test for our detection system."

Testing at a variety of sites is important because different environmental conditions affect how far and how fast seismic waves travel through the earth. That, in turn, affects how waves interact with buried mines and what kind of signal processing is required to image the mines.

The field tests have also given the researchers a chance to develop another aspect of the seismic mine detector—an audial representation of buried mines. "When the system passes over a mine, you hear a resonance that's easy to distinguish. What is an incident signal? It's a hollow sound like what you hear when you tap on a wall to find a stud," Scott explains, adding that the operator would listen to this resonance via a headset, or the unit would have a speaker. "In some cases, this audial representation was clearer than the visual representation."

As a result of this discovery, Georgia Tech will collaborate with CyTerra to evaluate the feasibility of incorporating the Georgia Tech seismic sensor into a handheld mine detector the company is producing for the U.S. Army. CyTerra's current handheld system combines a metal detector with ground-penetrating radar. "Integrating the capability that Georgia Tech has developed to acoustically measure vibrations will give us a triple-sensor device that should increase our ability to detect mines and reduce false alarms," says William Steinway, executive vice president of CyTerra, which is based in Waltham, Massachusetts.

"No single sensor has proven capable of detecting mines well with acceptable false alarms in all environmental conditions," Scott says, noting that what works best in a given situation depends on the type of mine and where it's buried. "A fusion of multiple sensors will most likely be necessary to get good performance in all conditions. Our seismic sensor is ideal to fuse with other types of sensors like GPRs and metal detectors."

In June 2003, researchers conducted their eighth field test in Skidaway Island, Georgia. This was the team's third visit to Skidaway, and data derived from this field test was consistent with earlier measurements—an encouraging result.

Even more important, researchers were able to test techniques for making the mine-detection system faster:

- *Shortening the acoustical signal.* In laboratory tests, researchers had been using a 4-second signal to displace the soil. "If you put more sound into the ground, the sound has more interaction with the mine. Yet you pay a penalty because it takes longer to measure," McCall explains. As field tests began, researchers encountered less background noise than they had in the lab, which enabled them to send a shorter signal. At Skidaway, researchers reduced the acoustical signal to one-sixteenth of a second and were still able to detect mines.

- *Continuous scanning.* With their current prototype system, researchers send a wave, take a measurement, then move the system 2 centimeters and repeat the process—a laborious task when measuring a square meter. At Skidaway, the researchers attempted to scan continuously, which accelerated the measuring process dramatically (by nearly 25 times) and still yielded good data.

"The positioner we used was never intended to do this, so with different hardware we should be able to get better results," says James S. Martin, a senior research engineer from Georgia Tech's School of Mechanical Engineering. "Even so, this was much better than the snail's pace at which we had been working."

Two radar sensors have been used in the current system to demonstrate that interactions between multiple sensors are not problematic. But adding more sensors would make the system faster. "Anytime you increase the number of sensors you're using, you can decrease the measurement time," says Gregg Larson, another School of Mechanical Engineering researcher on the project.

Bottom line, researchers say the time required to measure a square meter can be sliced from several hours to less than a minute. Faster measurements are crucial as the team develops a prototype for more extensive field tests. "We need to measure larger areas and gather more information about different mines, soil properties, and environmental conditions," Scott says, noting that data helps the researchers improve their numerical models and signal-processing algorithms. "Testing in different soil properties is important because the soil's complicated structure makes it too difficult to detect mines. You can't just look up the soil parameters we need in a book," he adds.

SEARCH AND RESCUE: AMRF-C STREAMLINING SHIPBOARD "ANTENNA FARMS"

Running out of space for new antennas on its ships, the U.S. Navy is turning to a new antenna design. In today's new world of network-centric warfare, where there's an ever greater dependence on vast amounts of information that must be received and transmitted, too many antennas are a growing shipboard problem. Antennas are heavy, "unstealthy," and tend to interfere with each other. Yet antennas are proliferating wildly because new radio systems, including radar, transmitters, receivers, and jammers, are continually entering service.

The demand for bandwidth in an age of information warfare isn't going away and the answer doesn't exist in limiting the use of the radio frequency spectrum. Ships, aircraft, even ground vehicles and individual marine infantry will all need more bandwidth in the years ahead. Instead, the solution lies in making antennas that can work with numerous RF-based devices.

To meet this need, managers of navy ship and aircraft programs are now looking at design work sponsored by the ONR that aims to develop an advanced multifunction radio-frequency concept (AMRF-C). The approach uses software to create common antenna apertures for multiple RF systems. AMRF-C eliminates the need for additional antenna hardware and would enable ship designers to dramatically pare back the microwave "antenna farms" that currently cover ships' topsides.

The AMRF-C effort will integrate radar and communications functions in a few sets of high-performance transmit and receive antenna apertures. Antenna growth—apart from the constantly increasing procurement and maintenance costs associated with individual "stovepipe" antenna types—has increased ships' radar cross-sections, making them more visible to enemy radar systems. The need for new antennas has also required extensive modifications in ship design to manage the added weight, as well as complex restrictions on use to minimize dangerous electronics interference. In addition to integrating radar and communications antennas, AMRF-C will support electronic warfare systems, which are designed to detect, jam, or deceive enemy radars and weapons.

"The AMRF-C effort aims at overcoming the antenna-proliferation crisis, with all the cost, ship-design, and operational problems this crisis creates," says Joe Lawrence, director of the ONR's surveillance, communications, and electronic combat division. "Instead of separate transmit and receive apertures for each of the multiple radar, communications, and electronic warfare systems, a few pairs of AMRF-C apertures would handle most microwave RF functions," he says.

The new concept addresses the design, systems-engineering, and maintenance problems that confront the developers of the navy's future surface ships. It also holds potential for businesses that must currently juggle multiple antennas on vehicles, buildings, and other man-made and natural structures.

THE HUMAN FACTOR

So far we've looked at numerous technologies that can help the military enhance its firepower and various support operations, but what about the people—soldiers and sailors—who make up the military? Can anything be done to improve their performance? You bet. The military is spending millions of dollars on cutting-edge research that will not only result in superior warfighters, but will help these brave people live more comfortably, even under the most adverse field conditions, and recover from wounds and injuries faster and with less pain. Chapter 4 focuses on the military's ongoing quest to create "fitter fighters."

CHAPTER FOUR

FITTER FIGHTERS

HEALTH, MEDICINE, AND BIOTECHNOLOGY

THE HEALTH AND FITNESS of troops have always been a major concern for military leaders. Until very recently, there wasn't much that could be done to help troops fight and feel better beyond providing adequate food, clothing, and shelter.

Until the twentieth century, more men were killed by disease and infection than by battle-related events. In the American Civil War, for example, 120,012 men were killed in action and 64,582 died of their wounds. A total of 186,216 soldiers died of a variety of different illnesses during the conflict. A big problem was that large numbers of soldiers came from rural areas and had not been exposed to common diseases such as chicken pox and mumps. Living in unhealthy conditions and often denied proper medical treatment, soldiers sometimes died of these diseases. For example, 5,177 soldiers in the Union Army died of measles during the war. Cases of smallpox, tuberculosis, and malaria were also rampant.

Contaminated food and water, including drinking from streams polluted by waste and corpses, also led to thousands of needless deaths. Union records show that diarrhea, typhoid, and dysentery claimed 35,127, 29,336, and 9,431 lives, respectively.

Today's military benefits from the great advancements made in medicine and public health over the past century and a half. Thanks to ongoing research, future generations of soldiers will receive even better treatment for wounds and illnesses, enhanced physical rehabilitation and reconstruction services, and improved comfort in the field. While war will always be hell, technology promises to at least ease some of the suffering, prevent many deaths, and help the wounded better recover from their injuries.

BUILDING BLOCK 1: GROWING BONE

Bone, often called the structural steel and reinforced concrete of the human body, supports the body the way a steel framework supports a skyscraper, and it protects its vital organs the way a cast-concrete roof protects its building's occupants. "Unfortunately, bone loss is an unavoidable consequence of aging, osteoporosis, and many traumatic accidents," says Carnegie Mellon University's Jeffrey Hollinger, who with his research team is developing a new therapy for regenerating bone.

To address the challenges of safe and effective therapy to restore form and function to deficient bone architecture, Hollinger's research team at Carnegie Mellon's Bone Tissue Engineering Center has developed an innovative therapy for growing bone by inserting a nonviral gene into the body to induce cells to grow bone.

"We are injecting the NTF gene into a site where bone is deficient via a synthetic hydro-gel made from a hyaluronic acid–based polymer," Hollinger says. "The hydro-gel/NTF is nonimmunogenic and is designed to restore form and function to bone deficiencies."

Some of the first preclinical trials will involve growing bone in the jaw, says Hollinger. (According to transportation officials, about 10 percent of vehicle accident injuries involve the jaw and the flat bones in the face.) "Restoring periodontal bone loss is a high priority for our team. And Bruce Doll, head of the periodontology department at the University of Pittsburgh is leading this challenge," Hollinger notes.

Through ever-improving surgical techniques, the replacement

of bone has been done via bone grafting either from the patient's own body or from animal (usually cow) bone. But because the human body is inclined to reject most "non-self" grafts, Hollinger's synthetic approach to growing bone will eliminate immune rejections. His research team includes Doll at the University of Pittsburgh's Dental School and Carnegie Mellon Bone Tissue Engineering Center scientists Yunhua Hu and Huihua Fu, the two scientists who perfected the NTF-hydrogel therapy, and whose work was the foundation for the NIH grant.

In addition to growing bone for injuries to the jaw, Hollinger's research team plans to use the new bone regeneration process to treat osteoporotic fractures, and in other applications for other parts of the body including the spine, pelvis, and all-powerful thigh bone—about 20 inches long and more than an inch across at the midshaft. A mature body contains more than 600 muscles and 206 bones, not counting the tiny sesamoid bones—like sesame seeds—embedded in the tendons of the thumb, big toe, and other pressure points.

"After blood, bone is the most frequently transplanted tissue. Current therapies for bone grafting fall short of the mark. The Bone Tissue Engineering Center is developing exciting new bone therapeutics that will offer surgeons and their patients much better options. And the NTF/injectable hydrogel is one such therapy from the Carnegie Mellon–Pitt team," says Hollinger.

BUILDING BLOCK 2: THE PLASTI-BONE

"Everyone told us this was a crazy idea," says Tony Mulligan of Advanced Ceramics Research (ACR) in Tucson, Arizona. "Only the Office of Naval Research said they'd take the chance."

When an arm or a leg bone is severely crushed, physicians usually cannot set it and bone grafts or amputation—until now—have remained the primary options. (The same is true for bones damaged by disease, such as cancer.) Mulligan's company, with ONR's help, has invented a process that may change all that.

If, for instance, the humerus bone in the arm is injured and damaged, ACR has shown that a CAT scan or MRI image can be made of the good arm bone, and converted to a "growth code"—a 3D virtual image—of the replacement bone segment needed. Using that data, ACR's rapid prototyping technology creates a microporous calcium phosphate–coated polymer "bone," which can be surgically implanted into the arm from which the damaged bone has been removed (Fig. 4–1).

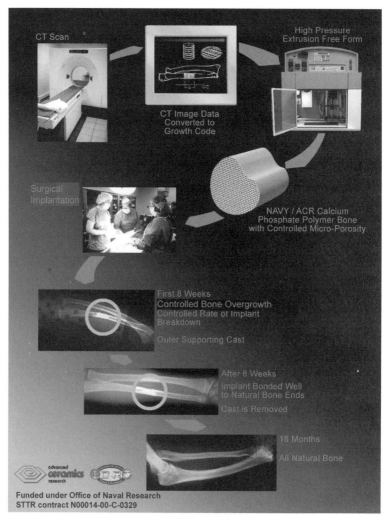

FIGURE 4–1.   CREATING PLASTIC BONE.

The calcium phosphate coating is very thin and allows the bone cells to attach to the implant. Growth factors could be added to the calcium phosphate to encourage the bone to grow at faster rates. "What is left of the real bone attaches itself to the polymer bone after about 8 weeks," says Ranji Vaidyanathan of ACR, inventor of the process. "Then, the real bone begins to 'grow through' the porous scaffold. As it does, it 'eats' the scaffold, and the body naturally excretes the calcium phosphate material. It is expected that within 18 months the bone will grow back completely, leaving the patient with natural bone." Proof that the process works has been shown in animal testing as well as in tissue cultures.

The project was funded by the Navy Small Business Technology Transition (STTR) program in the Office of Naval Research. ONR's manufacturing research motivated the topic, according to Ralph Wachter, an ONR science manager. ONR had been focusing on rapid creation of fully dense parts from metals and ceramics for defense needs, but decided to look for new applications and materials, believing that the technology offered the possibility of human health applications. Here, ACR has taken technologies originally developed for the rapid prototyping of military parts and transitioned them into applications that will have widespread use across the medical community.

"We decided on the dual-use area of bioengineering and tissue engineering in the navy's STTR program," says John Williams, the project's ONR program officer.

PREVENTIVE MEDICINE: TACKLING STRESS FRACTURES BEFORE THEY HAPPEN

Stress fractures caused by repetitive pounding activities of physical training take a toll on enough of the military population, especially recruits, that a major research program called "Bone Health and Medical Military Readiness" was started in 1997 to solve the problem.

The Bone Health and Metabolic Laboratory at the U.S. Army Research Institute of Environmental Medicine (USARIEM), located at the U.S. Army Soldier Systems Center in Natick, Massachusetts, using the latest research tools acquired in the past year, is ready to examine its piece of the stress fracture puzzle. "The goal of the whole program is to ultimately eliminate stress fractures," says Rachel Evans, a research physical therapist and director of bone health research. "Stress fracture cases have been reported since the late 1800s and today are one of the most common and potentially debilitating overuse injuries seen in military recruits, particularly in women."

Stress fractures occur when muscles transfer the overload of strain to the bone, most commonly the lower leg, which causes a tiny crack. They're tricky to see on an X-ray, but their impact on the military is large. They disrupt physical training, sideline troops, and cost the Defense Department as much as $100 million annually in medical costs and lost duty time, according to Evans.

Funded in part by Congress through the advocacy efforts of the National Coalition for Osteoporosis and Related Bone Diseases and the American Society for Bone and Mineral Research, and managed by USARIEM, the overall research is multifaceted, examining factors such as gait mechanics, impact attenuation, and genetics. USARIEM research physiologists are studying specifically how exercise and nutrition influence stress fractures. "A systematic approach to the study of stress fracture was needed but hadn't been done," Evans says. "With this focused effort, and recent breakthroughs in technology, we're hoping to come up with science-based strategies to identify individuals at risk for stress fracture, and then prevent their occurrence through innovative training interventions."

Karl Friedl, USARIEM commander, who earlier in his career led a study on bone health at Fort Lewis, Washington, says the understanding of bone physiology is significantly advancing and has widespread ramifications on health. "There has been no program in the DoD that paid attention to bone health in the past," Friedl says. "Anything we can provide has the potential to save millions of dollars and enhance readiness through reduction [of] lost duty time, attrition from the military, and medical cost avoidance. We want to avoid occupationally induced stress fractures now, and osteoporosis and osteoarthritis later."

Noninvasive methods of studying bone health at USARIEM started in the early 1990s with the first Dual Energy X-Ray Absorptiometry (DEXA) machine to measure bone density. Still in the lab, the older DEXA machines have been superseded by the superior software and scanning times in a new Prodigy fanbeam bone densitometer, according to Robert Mello, a research physiologist and lab director.

The Prodigy scans total body bone density in 5-inch instead of 1-inch increments, increasing precision and cutting scan time from 30 minutes to 6 minutes. Improved software provides a clearer picture of total body composition and bone mineral density. "We can look at regional areas of interest, such as sections of the tibia, forearm, or hip," Mello says. "[In the past] you had to scan an entire area. Just to have that capability is a major advance." The Prodigy also allows researchers to scan small animals for studies on bone health, Evans says.

While the Prodigy gives a front-to-back, two-dimensional view, the peripheral quantitative computerized tomography machine allows researchers to analyze 3D cross-sections of spongy and outer bone. It is designed to reconstruct a volumetric model of bone, from which bone density, and for the first time, bone geometry, can be determined. According to Evans, "We can now look at cross-sectional images where stress fractures are most common. There's also software to quantify muscle mass at that point."

Another scanning instrument is the handheld ultrasound bone sonometer, which examines bone quality by measuring the speed of sound of ultrasonic waves axially transmitted along the bone. The results aid in the assessment of bone strength. "We can identify bones that may be at risk," Mello says. "The big thing is the portability so that it can easily be taken to the field."

Although research is focused on preventing stress fractures in the military, Evans says what they learn can apply to any population of physically active people.

FASTER HEALING: HUMAN COLLAGEN WOUND DRESSING

A novel wound dressing made of genetically engineered human collagen that will enable faster and improved healing of injuries has been developed by researchers at the Hebrew University Faculty of Dental Medicine.

Collagen is the most abundant protein in the animal kingdom, including humans. It is the major constituent of connective tissues—tendons, skin, bones, cartilage, blood vessel walls, and membranes. Collagen fibers are the "warp and woof" of these connective tissues and are responsible for keeping all the body's organs and tissues in their correct functional structure. There are different collagen-containing preparations on the market today made for treating wounds, for use in dental implants, and in cosmetics. All of them use collagen made from animal tissues, which requires specific adaptation in order to eliminate immunological rejection or to prevent microbiological infection.

The dressing developed at the Hebrew University incorporates an inner layer of genetically engineered, human recombinant collagen. This material becomes a soluble, readily enzymatically degradable molecule in the wound tissue. The molecular fragments that are thus formed have been shown to play a pivotal role in the healing process. An outer layer, also of biological origin, is added to the wound dressing to provide initial protection prior to the release of the delicate collagen layer. Preliminary animal experiments with the new dressing have shown substantially faster and better healing, with rapid formation of new collagen fibers, than has been possible using older methods.

Although currently being developed privately, its ramifications for treating battlefield injuries are clear, and once it becomes available, military organizations worldwide will likely be very interested in using the new dressing. The new dressing is the result of many years of experimentation with collagen in the laboratory of Professor Emeritus Shmuel Shoshan of the Connective Tissue Research Laboratory of the Hebrew University Faculty of Dental Medicine. Shoshan is the inventor and chief scientist of Dittekol

Ltd., a company formed in cooperation with the Hebrew University's Yissum Research Development Company, to commercialize the new wound dressing. The company is now negotiating with investors for further development.

QUIKCLOT: AN END TO BLEEDING

If Michael Given of the ONR has his way, horrific scenes like those in Columbia Pictures' *Black Hawk Down* in which an Army Ranger in Somalia's Mogadishu bleeds to death after his buddies desperately try to clamp his gushing femoral artery wound, won't happen again.

Given knows the gruesome reality that 50 percent of troops wounded in the battlefield die before they are evacuated to field medical units because they hemorrhage to death (a statistic unchanged since the Civil War). He also knows that 50,000 Americans die each year at the site of auto accidents because of uncontrollable bleeding. As head of ONR's Casualty Care and Management program, Given is providing funding for research on a remarkable granular mineral compound called QuikClot, developed by Z-Medica, a small company located in Connecticut.

During tests in which severe arterial hemorrhage is treated with standard dressings, aggressive resuscitation, other hemostatic agents, or QuikClot, the latter turns wounds that once were 100 percent fatal into wounds that are 100 percent nonfatal. QuikClot is the only product or treatment to do so. In May 2002, just 14 days after the tests, these findings convinced the FDA to approve Quik-Clot for clinical use.

In 2002, with conflict looming in Afghanistan, QuikClot was sent overseas with the United Nations for use in their mine-clearing operations. Another 50,000 bagged units were shipped to Iraq. An injured serviceperson can self-administer the clotting powder (an account of a marine doing exactly that during the fighting in Iraq has been verified). The Department of Defense has confirmed reports of multiple uses of QuikClot in Iraq in which lives were saved, when used appropriately, and with no adverse effects. QuikClot is now becoming standard Marine Corps issue for every backpack first-aid kit.

Poured directly onto or into a wound after pressure is first applied, QuikClot absorbs all the liquid in the blood, and leaves behind the clotting factors. The material itself (refined zeolite) is indestructible. It can stay in the body until the injured person is removed to medical care, and it changes neither in size nor consistency when wound fluids are fully absorbed, rendering it easily irrigated or aspirated.

It only took 7 months for ONR to learn of QuikClot, test it, and get it deployed to U.S. troops. The product—already commercially available—is a remarkable medical advance for police and fire rescue units, EMTs, hikers, campers, and others far from local medical care. In 2004, QuikClot became available for home first-aid use. Z-Medica is also planning clinical trials to test anecdotal evidence that QuikClot could be helpful for the particular bleeding problems of diabetic and hemophiliac users.

SECOND SIGHT: RETINAL PROSTHESIS

Researchers from the Keck School of Medicine of the University of Southern California and its Doheny Retina Institute and Second Sight, LLC, are making progress on an intraocular retinal prosthesis that appears to be able to restore some degree of sight to the blind. Since vision damage is an all-too-common battlefield injury, the military is closely following the research's progress. "We have found that the devices are indeed electrically conducting, and can be used by the patients to detect light or even to distinguish between objects such as a cup or plate in forced choice tests conducted with one patient so far," says Mark Humayun, professor of ophthalmology at the Keck School.

The microelectronic retinal prosthesis is meant to stand in for the damaged retinal cells. The implant, which measures 4 millimeters by 5 millimeters, and is studded with sixteen electrodes in a four-by-four array, is a sliver of silicone and platinum that is often—but incorrectly—referred to as an "eye chip." Actually, it is attached to and sits atop the retina. It works by electrically stimulating the remaining healthy retinal cells via the array of electrodes; the retinal cells, in turn, pass on the visual information to the brain via the optic nerve. The device was developed by Sylmar, California–based Second Sight.

The first participant in the trial underwent surgery to receive the implant in February 2002, the second patient received the implant in July 2002, and the third patient underwent surgery in March 2003. Initial tests in the three implanted patients have shown that they can perceive light on each of the sixteen electrodes, and some of them were capable of detecting when a light is turned on or off, describing the motion of an object, and even counting discrete objects. As of this writing (late 2004), all of the patients reported varying degrees of restored vision.

The first tests of the prosthesis in all three patients involved computer-generated points of light sent directly to the implant, says Humayun. Over time, they were "graduated" to images received by an external video camera. These images are sent to the intraocular electrode array attached to the retina via a receiver that is implanted behind the patient's ear during the implant surgery. The signal is then recreated by stimulating the appropriate electrodes in the prosthesis.

Testing on the three patients is ongoing, says Humayun. "We plan in the near future to look at how useful the prosthesis can be in activities of daily living," he notes.

PERSONAL COOLERS: MICROCLIMATE CONTROL

Every soldier will carry some high-temperature relief when a microclimate cooling system is incorporated into the upcoming Objective Force Warrior uniform (see Chapter 1). Microclimate cooling has been researched and developed at the U.S. Army Soldier Systems Center in Natick, Massachusetts, since the 1980s, beginning with the Portable Vapor Compression System, a system shaped like a vacuum cleaner canister weighing 27 pounds,

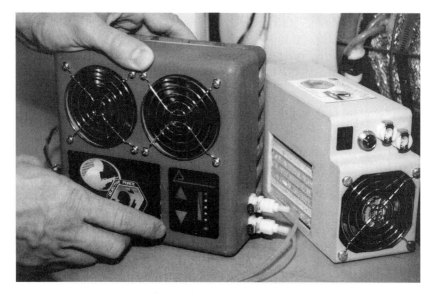

FIGURE 4–2.   PERSONAL COOLER PROTOTYPES.

leading now to a couple of prototype compact systems weighing less than 5 pounds that resemble an oversized brick (Fig. 4–2).

Engineers on the Chemical Technology Team are focused on having a system that weighs less than 4 pounds by 2008 and ultimately a system weighing less than 3 pounds by 2015 that will provide the desired cooling to enhance soldier safety and performance.

"Cooling is a medical and safety issue," says Brad Laprise, a mechanical engineer. "Comfort is a by-product. You'll never feel like you're in an air-conditioned room (with these systems), but the idea is to mitigate heat stress, allowing soldiers to do their jobs safely and more effectively."

Cooling can also be a force multiplier because troops can work longer without taking frequent breaks necessitated by high ambient temperatures. It also can reduce the logistics load by decreasing the amount of drinking water, says Walter Teal, a chemical engineer.

Microclimate cooling systems of various sorts are now used for different needs. In 1989, sailors aboard ships started wearing a vest that holds ice packs slipped into its horizontal pockets front and rear. Explosive Ordnance Disposal technicians and those encapsulated in outfits protecting them from toxic agent exposure use the Personal Ice Cooling System, which pumps ice-cold water from a 2-liter bottle carried by the individual through a tube-lined cooling garment. M1 tanks and Bradley infantry fighting vehicles have built-in systems that circulate filtered and conditioned air through a Natick-designed vest worn by members of the crew.

The latest application of microclimate cooling will benefit army helicopter pilots beginning in 2005, Laprise says. The initial Portable Vapor Compression System led to an intermediate unit weighing about 21 pounds, which was then developed in 1997 to a system weighing 6.6 pounds called the Advanced Lightweight Microclimate Cooling System, which eventually led to the Air Warrior Microclimate Cooling System program. Built into the helicopter, the system is worn with a new stitchless cooling garment (also designed at Natick). In testing, pilots using the cooling system could safely extend their mission from 1.6 hours to no less than 5.3 hours, according to Teal.

Still, what works for pilots in their aircraft isn't necessarily desirable for a dismounted soldier, which is why Laprise says it's impossible to have one microclimate system for everyone. The personal coolers designed by Aspen Systems in Marlborough, Massachusetts, and Foster-Miller in Waltham, Massachusetts, are unique prototypes using the same technology as the Advanced Lightweight Microclimate Cooling System but in a smaller package. "These prototypes are stepping stones. The next step is to take the lessons learned from the Aspen and Foster-Miller units and go to something smaller," Teal says. "We know we are pushing the envelope of vapor compression, but we think there are things we can do to lower the weight and power use."

Vapor compression technology works the same way as a refrigerator or air-conditioner. It's composed of a compressor, condenser, evaporator, thermal expansion tube, fan, and pump working to move heat to the ambient environment. In the case of microclimate cooling, liquid is chilled and pumped through a vest lined with a network of tubing, removing excess body heat.

The Foster-Miller prototype provides 110 watts of cooling at 95 F ambient temperature and weighs 4 pounds. The Aspen prototype weighs 4.65 pounds and provides 120 watts of cooling under the same conditions. Both require 50 watts of power, but engineers hope to achieve similar cooling capacity with only 30 watts in the future.

Although 300 watts of cooling is ideal, at least 100 watts of cooling is needed to lower core body temperature according to studies they've seen, Teal says. Lower cooling capacity is a trade-off for reduced weight. Shrinking size an inch or two and trimming a few ounces here and there will work for the next phase, but Teal says breakthrough technology is needed to achieve the most compact cooler for Objective Force Warrior. "Taking off those last 2 pounds will take more effort than the first 22 pounds," he says.

BETTER EATING THROUGH PLASMA

Some things never change. For instance, whether they're chowing down on K-rations, as in the mid-twentieth century, or Meals, Ready-to-Eat (MRE) packs, as today, troops will gripe about the taste of their grub. Often, the field dining critics are right, and the problem is typically related to the sterilization techniques that are used to preserve the food.

All packaged food must undergo sterilization, currently done using high temperatures or chemicals, both of which have drawbacks. Chemicals often leave a residue that can affect the safety and taste of the product, and produce undesirable waste as part of the processing. Heat is effective and rapid, but requires the use of costly heat-resistant plastics that can withstand sterilization temperatures. What if a new method could be found that eliminated the need for chemicals or heat-resistant plastics?

Plasma just might be the answer. At the U.S. Department of Energy's Princeton Plasma Physics Laboratory (PPPL), a team is conducting a small-scale research project studying plasma sterilization. This method, if successful, could be used to sterilize food and beverage containers, leading to an enormous savings—potentially hundreds of millions of dollars annually for a large soft drink manufacturer. "We have experiments indicating it is possible to kill microbes using a new plasma approach," noted John Schmidt, lead scientist of PPPL's Plasma Sterilization project. Schmidt cautioned, however, that the research is preliminary. "These experiments need to be published, peer reviewed, and repeated by other researchers to assure reliability. The physics research will be followed by considerable development work to arrive at a practical system for assembly-line use," says Schmidt, who has been awarded a patent for a plasma sterilization system.

To get started, PPPL researchers modified old equipment that had once been used to study RF waves for fusion applications. It consisted of a vacuum chamber equipped with an RF source, onto which a metal sphere measuring 1 inch in diameter was mounted at the center of the chamber. Before the experiment begins, the sphere is removed and sent to a commercial biological testing laboratory in Hightstown where a known number of *Bacillus subtilis* spores, a nontoxic microbe commonly used as a standard in lab testing, are placed on its surface. Following the experiment, the sphere is returned to Hightstown where technicians determine the number of spores killed in the process.

Fusion experiments at PPPL have generated plasmas with temperatures in the hundreds of millions of degrees centigrade. For killing spores, the PPPL researchers start with "low-temperature" hydrogen plasmas in the range of 50,000°C. At that temperature, the hydrogen ions are moving much too slowly to kill spores quickly; however, rapidly pulsing a 50-kilovolt potential between the sphere and the vacuum chamber solves the problem. The sphere is charged negatively and the vessel is at ground. Under these circumstances, the positively charged hydrogen ions accelerate toward the sphere in pulses energetic enough for the ions to pierce the hard outer shell and soft inner core of the spore. Recent experiments employed 4,000 ten-microsecond pulses, which reduced the population of live spores by a factor of 100:1000 (the kill ratio).

In the real world, sterilization time is precious, and equipment and processes suitable for the assembly line of a packaging plant would be needed. At present, RF generates a low-temperature hydrogen plasma inside the evacuated container, which is held in place by a surrounding conducting shell. An electrode is inserted into the container, and the plasma is then subjected to a pulsed differential of 50 kilovolts. The electrode is pulsed positively and the conducting shell is grounded. This causes the energized hydrogen ions to accelerate away from the electrode toward the conducting shell. On the way, they collide with the spores, which are present on the inner surface of the container. The hydrogen ions are energetic enough to penetrate the durable proteinaceous outer cover of the spores.

"These high-energy hydrogen ions stop very quickly and consequently deposit all their energy over a very small distance, a few microns, which, as it turns out, is the size of the spores. So, relatively modest currents of energetic hydrogen ions can do a large amount of damage inside the spores by messing up their DNA," says Schmidt. He estimates that a sufficient kill ratio could be attained by 10-microsecond pulses every millisecond for a period of a few seconds. Further experimentation is needed to confirm the number of 10-microsecond pulses necessary to reach the required kill ratio. A few seconds' processing time per container would make the system feasible for the assembly line.

The effectiveness of the hydrogen ions can be compared to that of gamma rays or X-rays used to sterilize bulk materials. Gamma and X-rays have long penetration depths, so they don't do as much damage per unit length as the hydrogen ions. "Textbooks contain the radiation-damage coefficients that are required to kill the relevant microbes. I am confident that we will be able to attain these," says Schmidt.

FIRST STRIKE RATION 1: NO STRIPPING, PLEASE

Stripping—getting rid of all but the most essential items from their prepackaged meal kits—is routine for ground troops that need to lighten the load they carry into battle. The new First Strike Ration (FSR) should minimize, if not eliminate, the task while bumping up the nutrition troops get for peak performance.

A development project of the DoD Combat Feeding Directorate, the FSR is a single-package, high-energy, no-utensils-required ration that would be substituted for three packages of the venerable MRE for forward-deployed troops in the first 72 hours of combat. "About 7 years ago, we said there has to be a better way to assess what items are being field-stripped, ensure that the remaining items contain the right nutrition level, and condense the cube," says Betty Davis, Performance Enhancement and Food Safety Team leader and project officer for the FSR.

Three MREs totaling 3,600 calories were being shaved to between 2,200 and 2,500 calories after soldiers tossed out the unwanted contents. Each FSR hits the target with about 2,300 calories, and is close to half the weight and volume of the MRE, which fits into the army's goal of becoming lighter, leaner, and more mobile as it transitions to the Objective Force Warrior. A positive side effect is that the FSR also reduces packaging waste.

When the concept was first created 2 years ago, the FSR was composed of breakfast, lunch, dinner, and snack pack, but Davis says the downfall was that each pouch opened the door to field-stripping. "Probably when the final version is in the field, soldiers will want to strip it; it's human nature, but in field tests, it has never been stripped," Davis says. "We have a great prototype FSR, but it's definitely going to be changing."

The latest prototype has proven so popular in tests that the U.S. Army Special Operations Support Command requested as many of the rations as the Combat Feeding employees could make in their Food Engineering Lab for shipment to Rangers deployed in support of Operation Iraqi Freedom. Every food was selected for its ability to be eaten out-of-hand by troops on the move. In its current form, the FSR is a single shrink-wrapped bag packed with a combination of familiar and new ration components. It now contains two shelf-stable pocket sandwiches, but, based on feedback, it will soon contain three; two flavors of miniature HooAH! nutritious booster bars; two servings of Energy Rich, Glucose Optimized

(ERGO) beverage mix; a dairy bar, crackers or bread, cheese spread, two sticks of beef jerky, a package of dried fruit, a modified version of applesauce named "Zapplesauce," a Ziploc bag, and an accessory packet missing the tiny bottle of Tabasco sauce but including an extra wet napkin.

Barbecue chicken and barbecue beef are the two varieties of pocket sandwiches now available, and Davis says that more varieties will be added as they are developed. The sandwiches are approved for the MRE and offer for the first time tidy sandwiches that don't require refrigeration. The dairy bar, likely to be renamed "dessert bar," is available in chocolate, peanut butter, mocha, banana nut, vanilla nut, vanilla, and strawberry flavors. The extruded bar, without a home since it was created about a decade ago, has the consistency of fudge and provides milk protein. "We took it off the shelf, revisited it, and made it cheaper to produce," says Davis. "A number of people here are excited about it, and it could find its way into other rations, including the MRE."

Zapplesauce is one of the best-liked components, according to Davis. The product is made with extra maltodextrin, a complex carbohydrate, for sustained energy release. Maltodextrin is also the key ingredient in ERGO, which tastes something like a sports drink. It's intended to increase endurance by conserving glycogen, which is energy stored in the liver and muscles. The ERGO drink packs will have a "fill-to" line so users easily know how much water to pour in.

Straws were desired, but are not feasible; therefore, other options, a spout for example, are being investigated for easier drinking and may be available as technology changes, says Davis. HooAH!, which is similar to commercial performance bars, comes in chocolate, peanut butter, apple-cinnamon, raspberry, and cran-raspberry flavors. HooAH! may be fortified with tyrosine or extra caffeine for performance enhancement, depending on test results with the U.S. Army Research Institute of Environmental Medicine. Other possibilities for the FSR include breakfast-type pocket sandwiches, a protein drink or bar, high-performance energy gel, and caffeinated sticks of gum.

The FSR has a shelf life of 2 (instead of 3) years at 80 F

because the rations don't have to be prepositioned (stored in advance). They have to stay warmer than 20 F to avoid freezing, and the soldier in the field will have to resort to another source to heat the food because, unlike the MRE, which contains a little chemical burner, no heater pack is included. The FSR is scheduled to be ready for fielding by 2007.

FIRST STRIKE RATION 2: POWER FUEL

Rapid yet sustained energy for troops could be a squeeze away with Power Fuel (Fig. 4–3), a quick energy booster gel in development at the DoD Combat Feeding Directorate. Power Fuel is part of Combat Feeding's Performance Enhancing Delivery System, a military food system that will deliver performance-enhancing natural food to troops in the field.

Energy gels in the commercial market are popular with athletes, who want easily absorbed and digested carbohydrate-based calories to replace glucose expended during a workout or race. Packaged in plastic pouches, the 1-ounce servings are sucked out

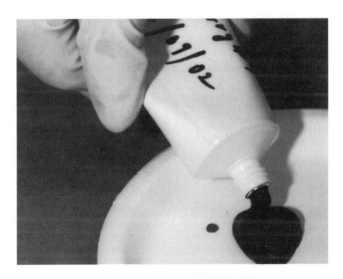

FIGURE 4–3.   POURING POWER FUEL.

on the move and out of hand. Troops engaged in high physical activity might also benefit from such a product, and food technologists are taking the gel formulation to another level. "The more motivated ones [troops or athletes] are going to want to do anything to get a performance advantage," says Jack Briggs, a food technologist on the Performance Enhancement and Food Safety Team.

The gels apparently have staying power as well, according to a study completed this year by the U.S. Army Research Institute of Environmental Medicine. The study compared the responses of human volunteers after consuming glucose water, a highly viscous glucose gel (the control product), and Combat Feeding's finished gel product. All three have equal carbohydrate content.

The finished gel, which contains a mixture of glucose and maltodextrin—a complex carbohydrate—along with fat and a trace of protein, showed significant improvement over both the glucose water and high-viscosity glucose, but, according to Briggs, the most interesting finding was the gel's biphasic characteristic, which means that, after reaching its apex or "glucose spike" and then decreasing, the glucose levels in six of the thirteen participants rebounded and slightly increased for a period of time instead of continuing to decrease to baseline levels or lower, which is typically the case. "None of us can understand it. We've never seen it before, but it appears you can get another boost of energy," Briggs says. "You . . . get a slower absorption of glucose initially but the release of glucose to the bloodstream [is] sustained for a longer period of time. We feel very confident that modulating glucose uptake and release will maintain energy levels and potentially improve soldier performance in the field." The next step is to further explore that characteristic of glucose modulation. What is learned may be applied to other military rations.

Still, how it works won't matter if the gel is unsavory. Taste was evaluated in sensory panels with exercisers and other consumers familiar with commercial gels, and the Power Fuel had a good overall acceptance compared to the four products on the market, according to Briggs. Current flavors are mixed berry, apple-cinnamon, cherry vanilla, and mocha. The gel is created from juice concentrates (except for mocha, which includes caffeine), various carbohydrates, unsaturated fats, and gums. Other performance-enhancing ingredients, such as tyrosine or glutamine, may fortify the gel if they prove effective, says Briggs.

By comparison, some commercial gels are basically corn/rice syrup and flavoring, and they aren't required to have a minimum shelf life of 3 years at 80 F or 6 months at 100 F. Packaged in a capped tube, Power Fuel's serving size of 3.4 ounces delivers from 240 calories to 320 calories, depending on the flavor, and is about 3 times the portion of commercial gels. The gels are also being tested in a pouch. According to Briggs, the army's goal is to make Power Fuel commercially available to hold down costs. If approved for the military, Power Fuel will be issued as part of the First Strike Ration, which is scheduled for release in 2007.

REFUELING: EASY-TO-USE DRINK POUCHES

Field data show that about half of the soldiers don't bother preparing the beverage contained in the MRE because using and cleaning the canteen cup is inconvenient (pouring the mix into a canteen full of water is prohibited by the army), reports Lauren Milch, a physical scientist at Combat Feeding, who managed package development.

Drink pouches developed by the DoD Combat Feeding Directorate at the U.S. Army Soldier Systems Center in Natick, Massachussets, in partnership with packaging companies Pactech in Rochester, New York, and Kapack in Minneapolis, Minnesota, allow soldiers to pour water into a package containing a powder mix, shake it, and drink the beverage directly from the pouch, which can be rezippered for later use.

The 12-ounce beverage pouch is the first project of the Individual Combat Ration Team's improved packaging program, which is aimed at reducing packaging and increasing consumption, says Vicki Loveridge, a senior food technologist and project officer for improved packaging. Including a resealable plastic bag was a partial solution, but, by replacing the current dry mix package with a disposable drinking vessel, the drink pouch takes care of everything.

Originally intended to replace the MRE beverage base mix, the beverage pouches could be used for any of the military ration beverages or liquid foods, including hot drinks, because the pouch is designed to fit into a flameless ration heater. A rectangular drink pouch with a plastic zipper was evaluated in 1991, but it was shelved because the cost (25 cents apiece) was considered "extravagant."

In the last 3 years researchers developed prototype pouches with a nonreclosable tear-off spout, reclosable sports-type pull cap, and a twist-off cap that were studied along with the final package design. "We wanted something reusable, [it] didn't . . . need to stand up, [but there had to be] a way to set it down," Loveridge says. "The extra expense of a stand-up pouch was unnecessary, and it's a harder pouch to keep from cracking."

In the first evaluation using a pouch with a twist-off cap in 2001, 91 percent of the troops consumed their beverages, but the twist-off cap was too bulky and expensive. The latest prototype has a tear-off strip just above a resealable interlocking plastic zipper on top. Its slight hourglass shape makes it easy to hold. "What's very different from what you see at the grocery store is the zipper with a multilaminate foil and 3-year shelf life," Loveridge says. "It's difficult to incorporate a zipper without compromising the foil."

Four studies already conducted show substantial increases in the number of troops using the beverage pouch; another field test is scheduled to determine how fighter performance improves with increased hydration.

An order of 7,000 beverage pouches has been placed for two Combat Feeding developmental products, the Remote Unit Self Heated Meal and First Strike Ration, according to Loveridge. An electrolyte-based drink powder beverage pouch was approved for four varieties of the 2004 MRE menu.

"The drink pouch is something they really need, and it's designed to add minimal cost," Milch says.

INTO THE TUB: ENVIRONMENTAL IMPACT STUDIES

If the 14-foot depth of the Water Immersion Laboratory tank at the U.S. Army Research Institute of Environmental Medicine (USARIEM) seems excessive, there's a good reason for it.

Researchers at USARIEM, located at the U.S. Army Soldier Systems Center in Natick, Massachusetts, have been using the laboratory to evaluate human responses to cold or hot environments since the USARIEM building was constructed in 1968. Renovated in 2000, the lab's premier feature is its 10-foot by 10-foot stainless steel tank filled with 10,000 gallons of chlorinated water. "Visitors are always surprised at how deep it is, but once [the water] gets to temperature, we can keep it at that temperature within a few tenths of a degree," says John Castellani, a research physiologist in USARIEM's Thermal and Mountain Medicine Division. "That's the benefit of a deep tank."

In addition to the depth of the tank, the facility is unusual for its ability to test humans exercising on an underwater treadmill or stationary bike—while sitting on bolted-down stainless steel chairs, with two cycle ergometers, each of which has a moveable plate system to adjust to individual leg length. The resistance is adjusted by attaching or removing fins to the wheel.

Each of the exercise machines is independently operated and raised or lowered on separate platforms into the water, which has an operational temperature range of 41 to 122 F (most human exposures in the test protocols range from 59 to 104 F). Human research volunteers are connected to a data acquisition system, a nearby computer on the platform that surrounds the tank and records the subject's physiological status.

In recent years, research has focused on cold temperatures. Nearly 5 years ago, a commercial hot tub was acquired as a re-warming pool to help test subjects raise their body temperature quickly after soaking in chilly water. "We're interested in how hypothermia affects humans," says Castellani. "This facility works out well because it gives you a great place to recreate a cold or cold-wet environment." Water takes away heat 25 times faster than air, which makes it easier for researchers to reduce core body temperature without risking a cold injury that could occur in an air chamber, he observes.

They were motivated to study hypothermia after four Army Rangers died while going through training at Eglin Air Force Base, Florida, in 1995. Scientists used the water immersion lab along with the climatic chambers to pursue research on how cooling affects performance. A "repeated immersion" study in 1996–1997 simulated what happens when a soldier enters the water for 2 hours at a time, three times per day. By the second and third immersion, researchers learned that body temperatures decreased because the test subjects could not shiver as well as they had the first time.

Researchers also used the facility to determine if exercise fatigue causes thermoregulatory fatigue. Volunteers exercised or remained motionless in the water, which was then followed by cold air exposure. Those exercising and fatigued had a lower body temperature because they could not retain their body heat as well as those who had been motionless. "The idea is to feed data into our cold [temperature] models. We're trying to add fatigue factors into the existing model, which is now good, but we're building on it," says Castellani.

The treadmill, a relatively new addition, is helpful because it can simulate wading in a swamp, which is more realistic than the cycle, says Castellani. Researchers can vary the treadmill speed, water temperature, and, by raising or lowering the platform, the water depth to test responses at different points along the body.

A study that has just begun is looking at how long people can stay in water at different depths and temperatures. A second part of the study will take volunteers, whose temperature has been reduced, into a cold chamber to test their cognitive and physical performance through a series of Special Operations Command tests. "We don't have much information on this at the temperatures and depths we're looking at," says Castellani. "We've been able to understand that stressors soldiers undergo [degrade] thermal regulation. That information will help us design better physiological models." Ultimately, the goal is to predict under what conditions a soldier declines in performance and may become a casualty, he said, giving troops the information to make the right decisions and avoid harm.

Work in the facility has been wide ranging. For example, the lab helped validate the core body temperature pill against conventional methods of measuring body temperature.

BRAIN–MACHINE INTERFACES

Devices including "neuroprosthetic" limbs for paralyzed people and "neurorobots" controlled by brain signals from human operators could be the ultimate applications of brain–machine interface technologies developed under a $26 million contract to Duke University sponsored by DARPA and part of its Brain–Machine Interfaces Program, which seeks to develop new technologies for augmenting human performance by accessing the brain in real time and integrating the information into external devices.

Principal investigator for the DARPA project will be a professor of neurobiology, Miguel Nicolelis. Coprincipal investigators are Craig Henriquez, who is the W.H. Gardner Jr. Associate Professor of Biomedical Engineering; a professor of neurosurgery, Dennis Turner; and associate professor of biomedical engineering, Patrick Wolf. Other center collaborators include John Chapin of the State University of New York—Brooklyn, Jose Principe of the University of Florida, Mandayam Srinivasan of Massachusetts Institute of Technology, and Harvey Wiggins of Plexon in Dallas.

The DARPA support will help launch Duke's Center for Neuroengineering, codirected by Nicolelis and Henriquez, whose scientists and engineers will seek to pioneer a new technological era in which brain signals control machines that augment and extend human capabilities in a way never before possible. In addition to the development of brain-controlled prosthetic limbs, neurosurgeons could apply brain-mapping enabled by the new technologies to aid in distinguishing healthy brain tissue from that which is part of a tumor or a focus for epileptic seizures.

"This technology can immediately increase the resolution with which surgeons can map the extent of a tumor or a specific brain region," said Nicolelis. "Such improved mapping can translate into a better prognosis for the patient, since less tissue might have to be removed." Beyond medical uses, brain–machine interfaces also could be applied to enhance the abilities of normal humans; for example, neurally controlled robots could enable remote search-and-rescue operations or the exploration of hazardous or inaccessible environments.

The Duke Center will consist initially of a collaboration of separate laboratories in the medical center's department of neurobiology and in the Pratt School of Engineering's department of biomedical engineering. However, the researchers expect to unite the centers' efforts in a new multidisciplinary engineering building now under construction. As part of the DARPA support:

- Biomedical engineer Henriquez and his colleagues will coordinate development of equipment and methods for visualizing and analyzing the massive amounts of data produced from electrode arrays in the brains of experimental animals.

- Neurosurgeon Turner and his colleagues will investigate potential uses of brain–machine interfaces in patients with neurological disorders.

- Biomedical engineer Patrick Wolf and his colleagues will develop a miniaturized "neurochip" for detecting and analyzing brain signals, as well as optical communications links between the chip and the control components of the interface.

- John Chapin's laboratory will develop the sensory feedback mechanism by which animals and humans can "feel" the actions of a neurorobotic arm or hand.

- Jose Principe and his colleagues will develop new computer algorithms for translating brain-derived signals into control commands to operate a robot arm.

■ Mandayam Srinivasan's laboratory will develop new interfaces to provide visual and tactile feedback signals to animal subjects operating robot arms, and Harvey Wiggins will supply hardware and software that will enable development and testing of brain–machine interfaces.

According to Nicolelis, based on the success of initial experiments with animals, the new center will begin by concentrating on neuroprosthetic arms for paralyzed people.

"[A few years after the research was conducted], we reported experiments in primates showing that a brain–machine interface could, indeed, control a robot arm," says Nicolelis. "While this was a first-generation system, it proved to us that there was an enormous opportunity to pursue research leading to clinical applications. We are extremely grateful to DARPA for their vision in establishing a program that will provide the crucial support to launch this effort."

In 2000, Nicolelis and his colleagues tested a neural system on monkeys that enabled the animals to use their brain signals, as detected by implanted electrodes, to control a robot arm to reach for a piece of food. The scientists are even able to transmit the brain signals over the Internet, remotely controlling a robot arm 600 miles away. The technique, called multineuron population recordings, was originally developed by Chapin.

In the experiments, the scientists used arrays of up to ninety-six electrodes to sense signals from multiple areas of the brain, including the motor cortex, which controls movement. The scientists recorded the output of these electrodes as the animals learned reaching tasks, which included reaching for small pieces of food. They then fed the mass of neural signal data generated during many repetitions of these tasks into a computer, which analyzed the brain signals to detect telltale patterns that would enable researchers to predict the trajectory of the monkey's hand from the signals. By programming the computer connected to the robotic arm to sense the signal patterns emanating from the monkey's brain, the monkey, in effect, controlled the arm via neural signals. This proof-of-concept experiment showed the effectiveness of recording from multiple areas of the brain and then allowing the computer to "learn" brain signal patterns that triggered certain movements.

In the new center, Nicolelis, Henriquez, and their colleagues will aim to increase the number of recording electrodes to more than 1,000 to enable more complex actions by robotic arms and other devices. The neurochip being developed by Wolf and his colleagues will greatly reduce the size of the circuitry required for sampling and analysis of brain signals.

"Our dream is to develop a palmtop-like device that routes the signals either to robotic devices, computers, or even to the physician, to alert the physician to some problem," says Nicolelis. According to Henriquez, the greater number of recording electrodes will also enable far more sophisticated analyses of brain signals: "This research involves a major effort to decode how the brain manages information. Once we are able to use computation to decode such information, we can translate that understanding into an algorithm that can be incorporated into hardware."

Ultimately, the researchers hope to record and analyze such signals for long periods of time without damage to brain tissue. They have already shown that animals can tolerate the electrodes for periods of years without apparent harm. According to Nicolelis, the technology and computational methods developed with DARPA's support will also lead to a deeper understanding of the brain itself.

"This research will provide us with a powerful new set of experimental tools and techniques to answer the question of how millions of brain cells come together to generate a particular behavior," he says. "Traditionally, the neurosciences have taken a reductionist approach, with investigators trying to understand individual neurons, molecules, and genes. We are trying to understand the brain's function as a dynamic system."

Nicolelis, Henriquez, and their colleagues are among researchers developing a theory that neurons are not hard-wired circuit elements permanently assigned to one computing task, like the microprocessor inside a computer. Rather, the new theory holds that neurons are adaptable, living entities that can participate in many processing tasks at once. Moreover, the theory holds that those tasks may change from millisecond to millisecond. For example, Nicolelis's experiments have revealed that the brain signals producing a single event, such as a monkey reaching out, are mirrored in many places in the same brain region, almost as if the neurons vote on such actions.

In their current experiments, the center's scientists and engineers are developing closed-loop systems, in which movement of the robot arm generates tactile feedback signals in the form of pressure on the animals' skin. They are also providing visual feedback to the animal by allowing it to watch the movement of the arm. Such feedback studies could potentially improve the ability of paralyzed people to use such a brain–machine interface to control prosthetic appendages, says Nicolelis. In fact, the brain could prove extraordinarily adept at using feedback to adapt to such an artificial appendage.

"One provocative, and controversial, question is whether the brain can actually incorporate a machine as part of the neural representation of the body," he says. "I truly believe that it is possible. The brain is continuously learning and adapting, and previous studies have shown that the body representation in the brain is dynamic. So, if you create a closed feedback loop in which the brain controls a device and the device provides feedback to the brain, I would predict that as people or animals learn to use the device, their brains will basically dedicate neuronal space to represent that device."

Development of the Duke Center's brain-interface technologies also will involve collaboration with industry, say the researchers. The market for such devices should be considerable.

"In our discussion with corporations, we've found that, even though these technologies are in their infancy, the companies are emphasizing their commercial development," says Henriquez. "We believe that the Duke Center will help propel development of the next generation of brain-interface technologies. And the opportunities for their application seem almost boundless."

The military's interest in this research is far reaching—and even a little bit scary. If perfected, brain-interface technology would allow pilots to fly planes and other vehicles—both manned and unmanned—merely by thinking commands. Taken a step further, it's not inconceivable to envision a world in which missiles, torpedoes, rockets—even bullets—are guided by thought. In such a world, it would be literally possible to wish somebody dead.

BLEEX: STRENGTH-ENHANCING EXOSKELETON

The mere thought of hauling a 70-pound pack across miles of rugged terrain or up fifty flights of stairs is enough to evoke a grimace in even the burliest individuals. But breakthrough robotics research at the University of California—Berkeley could soon bring welcome relief—a self-powered exoskeleton to effectively take the load off soldiers' backs.

"We set out to create an exoskeleton that combines a human control system with robotic muscle," says Homayoon Kazerooni, professor of mechanical engineering and director of Berkeley's Robotics and Human Engineering Laboratory. "We've designed this system to be ergonomic, highly maneuverable, and technically robust so the wearer can walk, squat, bend, and swing from side to side without noticeable reductions in agility. The human pilot can also step over and under obstructions while carrying equipment and supplies."

The Berkeley Lower Extremity Exoskeleton (BLEEX) (Fig. 4–4), as it's officially called, consists of mechanical, metal leg braces that are connected rigidly to the user at the feet, and, in order to prevent skin abrasion, less tightly elsewhere. The device includes a power unit and a backpack-like frame used to carry a large load.

Equipment like this could become an invaluable tool for anyone who needs to travel long distances by foot with a heavy load. The exoskeleton could eventually be used by army medics to

FIGURE 4–4.   BERKELEY LOWER-EXTREMITY EXOSKELETON.

carry injured soldiers off a battlefield, by firefighters to haul their gear up dozens of flights of stairs to put out a high-rise blaze, or by rescue workers to bring in food and first-aid supplies to areas where vehicles cannot enter. "The fundamental technology developed here can also be developed to help people with limited muscle ability to walk optimally," says Kazerooni.

The researchers point out that the user does not need a joystick, button, or special keyboard to "drive" the device. Rather, the machine is designed so that the pilot becomes an integral part of the exoskeleton, and, therefore, no special training is required to use it. In the UC—Berkeley experiments, the person moved about a room wearing the 100-pound exoskeleton and a 70-pound backpack, but felt as if he were carrying a mere 5 pounds.

The project, funded by DARPA, began in earnest in 2000. For the current model, the user steps into a pair of modified army boots that are then attached to the exoskeleton. A pair of metal legs frames the outside of a person's legs to facilitate movement. The wearer then dons the exoskeleton's vest, which is attached to the backpack frame and engine. If the machine runs out of fuel, the exoskeleton legs can be easily removed so that the device converts to a large backpack.

More than forty sensors and hydraulic actuators form a local area network (LAN) for the exoskeleton and function much like a human nervous system. The sensors, including some that are embedded within the shoe pads, are constantly providing the central computer brain information so that it can adjust the load based upon what the person is doing. When it is turned on, the exoskeleton is constantly calculating what it needs to do to distribute the weight so little or no load is imposed on the wearer "in order to make this as practical and robust as possible," says Kazerooni. "Several engineers around the world are working on motorized exoskeletons that can enhance human strength, but we've advanced our design to the point where a pilot could strap on the external metal frame and walk in figure eights around a room. No one else has done that."

One significant challenge for the researchers was to design a fuel-based power source and actuation system that would provide the energy needed for a long mission. The Berkeley researchers are using an engine that delivers hydraulic power for locomotion and electrical power for the computer. The engine provides the requisite energy needed to power the exoskeleton while affording ease of refueling in the field.

The current prototype allows a person to travel over flat terrain and slopes, but work on the exoskeleton is ongoing, with the focus turning to miniaturization of its components. The UC—

Berkeley engineers are also developing a quieter, more powerful engine and a faster, more intelligent controller that will enable the exoskeleton to carry loads up to 120 pounds. In addition, the researchers are studying what it takes to enable pilots to run and jump with the exoskeleton legs. The engineers point out that while the exoskeleton does the heavy lifting, the operator contributes to the balance. "The pilot is not driving the exoskeleton," says Kazerooni. "Instead, the control algorithms in the computer are constantly calculating how to move the exoskeleton so that it moves in concert with the human."

Appropriately enough, the first step in the project began with researchers analyzing the human step. They gathered information about how people walk and move, including the propulsive force and torque needed from the ankles and the shock-absorbing power of the knees, so they could adapt the exoskeleton to a wide range of natural human movements. "Many scientists and engineers have been attempting to build a robotic strength-enhancing device since the 1950s, and they've failed," says Kazerooni. "It is only through recent engineering breakthroughs that this dream is now becoming a reality."

LOW-TECH SOLUTION/HIGH-TECH SAVINGS: TENT WARMERS

At first glance, the self-powered thermoelectric fan (Fig. 4–5) used with the army's family of space heaters may appear to be a high-priced air mover. However, when used with nonelectric space heaters, the fan/tent heater combination is the most inexpensive option available to army units for temporary space heating, costing several thousand dollars less than electric-powered, forced hot air systems.

The fan was conceived and developed by the Shelters Team of the Product Manager–Force Sustainment Systems as an important accessory to space heaters that operate on liquid or solid fuel. It is manufactured by Aspen Systems in Marlborough, Massachusetts.

FIGURE 4–5.   TENT WARMER.

In uninsulated structures, such as tents and barracks, the forces of natural convection are so strong that air heated by the stove quickly rises to the ceiling, leaving the area near the floor much colder. With the fan, heated air is circulated downward, creating more even heat distribution.

Testing conducted in the Soldier Systems Center arctic chamber at −60 F showed that the fan can increase the temperature 1 foot off the floor by more than 20 F. This is important because soldiers sleep on or near the floor, and the most difficult part of the body to keep warm is the feet. "With the fan we can have the stove barely on and it will warm you throughout the tent, whereas before you had to be right on the stove to stay warm, and your backside was still cold," says Chris Harder in Fort Gordon, Georgia. "I wish I had these in my unit over in Korea. It would make a huge change in wintertime comfort."

When placed on a heater surface, the self-powered fan converts a small amount of heat energy directly into electricity to drive the fan's impeller. It improves the performance of the heater by creating warmth throughout a larger area with the same fuel consumption, or it can heat the same area with less fuel. Reduced fuel consumption, primarily JP-8 or diesel, is an important advantage because fuel must be transported along with the field unit, costing the army as much as $15 to $23 per gallon.

Fuel use is critical to the army because fueling stations are remote in a combat zone. For this reason, logistic fuel is considerably more important than ammunition at every point along the battlefield except at the leading edge of the fighting, and even there, from time to time, fuel is more highly valued, according to Paul Kern, U.S. Army Materiel Command commander, speaking at the Society of Automotive Engineers World Congress in March 2003. In cold climates, the army has estimated that a single fan can save as much as 320 gallons of heating oil in one heating season. Actual results depend on the local climate and annual "degree-days," which is the difference between 65 F and the day's average temperature. Since the fan's introduction in 2000, the Defense Logistics Agency (DLA) has received orders for more than 6,000 fans.

ROLLING ALONG

Napoleon is reported to have said that an army travels on its stomach. That, to a certain extent, is true. But an army also travels on planes, ships, buses, trucks, and numerous other types of vehicles. Moving troops and supplies quickly, efficiently, and safely is as important to today's military leaders as it was to officers during the Napoleonic Wars. And just as horses and sailing vessels eventually gave way to motor vehicles, airplanes, and motorized ships, today's transportation modes are destined to yield to an upcoming generation of high-tech mobility and logistics systems.

CHAPTER FIVE

MOVING AHEAD

VEHICLES AND LOGISTICS

MOVING TROOPS, EQUIPMENT, supplies, and munitions from one place to another quickly and efficiently has always been a top priority for military leaders. More than one battle has been lost simply because a commander failed to direct critical resources to a key location. Transportation, in the form of delivery systems, also enables the delivery of tactical weapons to their targets.

Transportation and technology have always been partners. Whether designing a better chariot or jet fighter, researchers have strived to create vehicles that move faster and quieter, and are more efficient, safe, and stealthy than their predecessors. This trend shows no sign of diminishing anytime soon.

ELECTRICAL SIGNAL ANALYSIS KEEPS PLANES IN THE AIR

A new instrument developed at Oak Ridge National Laboratory allows mechanics to know in seconds if a fuel pump of a military transport plane like the C-141 Starlifter is excessively worn and could fail.

That information is vital to maintaining combat readiness,

which is especially important with today's conditions, says Don Welch, a codeveloper of the instrument and a researcher in the Department of Energy's Engineering Science and Technology Division. "[Although] the C-141 has twenty fuel pumps, if even one is bad it may ground the plane," Welch says. "[Using] this tool is a crucial first step in identifying operating fuel pumps that are on the verge of failure." The payoff is increased reliability and maintenance efficiency of the C-141, regarded as the workhorse of the air force's Air Mobility Command. The plane, powered by four turbofan engines, can haul 200 soldiers, 155 paratroopers, or nearly 69,000 pounds of cargo.

The instrument is a personal computer–based system with menu-driven software and is housed in a rugged case that fits within the size restrictions of carry-on luggage. The unit is battery powered and can be used either in the hangar or on the flight line by maintenance personnel. "Our system measures changes in the electric current drawn by a motor as an indicator of changes in the mechanical load that it is driving," says Howard Haynes, one of the technology's developers. "In this case, the changes in current reflect wear in either the pump or motor assembly." By using the instrument, mechanics can (remotely and in harsh environments such as those that prevail in the C-141, where the pumps are submerged in the fuel) identify wear in the fuel pump that has exceeded allowable tolerances.

Test results of prototype systems on C-141s have been extremely positive, and ORNL has already turned over two prototypes to the air force. In addition, the technology has a number of other applications: It has been shown to be an effective tool for diagnosing adverse conditions of rotor and gear train in helicopters, army portable power generators, navy fire and seawater pumps, NASA propellant control valves, heat pump and air-conditioning systems, air compressors, army ammunition delivery systems, diesel engine starter motors, and electric vehicle motors and alternators.

Haynes and colleagues trace the roots of electrical signature analysis to work in the mid-1980s for the Nuclear Regulatory Commission to monitor aging and service wear of nuclear power plant motor-operated valves. Then, the goal was to develop diagnostic techniques that used the motor's running current because they could acquire it remotely and nonintrusively. The techniques provided a breakthrough in detecting load and speed variations generated anywhere within the motor-operated valves by converting them into signatures that reveal problems and potential failures. Electrical signature analysis now includes current, voltage, and power analysis.

SILENCERS: QUIETER JET ENGINES

Jet engines may run quieter in the future, with technology developed at Ohio State University (OSU), where researchers have developed a silencer technology that creates electrical arcs to control turbulence in engine exhaust airflow—the chief cause of engine noise. Until recently, noise was a problem only for commercial airports, which are often surrounded by residential areas, but as populations spread around the United States, military airports have also started to feel pressure from neighboring communities to reduce noise from their planes.

Furthermore, from a military standpoint, the silencers—called plasma actuators—developed for noise mitigation could also provide an additional level of stealth for modern military aircraft. Pilots could fire the electrical arcs in certain patterns to mix the very hot exhaust gas with outside air, significantly reducing the heat signature that shows up on infrared tracking systems.

Using the new technology, with the flip of a switch, pilots could turn the silencers on and off, reducing noise around commercial airports or military airstrips, according to Mohammad Samimy, an OSU professor of mechanical engineering. He and his colleague, Igor Adamovich, an associate professor of mechanical engineering, demonstrated the technology in a series of laboratory tests in which they used laser light to illuminate a simulated engine exhaust stream, and studied how different arrangements of actuators affected the flow. The university has applied for a patent on the design.

The researchers tested the actuators using two types of airstreams: one simulating the exhaust from a commercial aircraft, and the other simulating that of a high-speed military aircraft. Typical large commercial aircraft, such as the Boeing 747, fly at Mach 0.85, or 0.85 times the speed of sound, while modern military aircraft can top Mach 2. The tests showed that the plasma actuators succeeded in manipulating turbulence structures in the airflow. All jet aircraft could benefit from the technology, Samimy says.

The most important factor in silencing an aircraft during takeoff—when the jet engine is the loudest—is controlling exhaust airflow, since it is the high-speed airflow that provides thrust for the plane, but also creates most of the noise. "One has to reduce the noise while not adversely affecting the thrust—that is the challenge. When the development of the actuators is complete, they will meet the challenge," Samimy adds.

Samimy studies turbulence as part of his work with fluid dynamics, one of the most complex areas of study in science and engineering. Flow control is a multidisciplinary subject, which draws researchers from areas such as mechanical, aeronautical, and electrical engineering. By analyzing images of fluid flows, Samimy and his colleagues can gather a wealth of information that can be used in controlling the flow. They can, for example, tune the newly developed plasma actuators to match certain frequencies in the flow and optimize noise reduction.

This project grew out of Samimy's work for NASA in the 1990s in which he worked on structural modifications at the trailing edge of the exhaust system called tabs or chevrons—zigzag-shaped cutouts at the nozzle exit thereby affecting the engine's noise characteristics. Some of the most recent aircraft engines contain chevrons.

While chevrons reduce noise, they lower fuel efficiency, and although chevrons are only needed during takeoff and landing, they are permanent fixtures of the engine and cannot be disengaged at cruise altitude to increase fuel efficiency. "I wanted to design actuators that could [be turned] on and off and exploit instabilities in the flow," Samimy says. "Plasma actuators are those kinds of actuators."

SHAPE SHIFTER: BIRDLIKE/FISHLIKE AIRPLANE WINGS

To maximize a plane's efficiency over a broader range of flight speeds, Penn State engineers, with the support of NASA and DARPA, have developed a concept for morphing airplane wings that change shape like a bird's and are covered with a segmented outer skin like the scales of a fish.

George Lesieutre, a professor of aerospace engineering who leads the project, says, "Airplanes today are a design compromise. They have a fixed-wing structure that is not ideal for every part of a typical flight. Being able to change the shape of the wings to reduce drag and power, which vary with flight speed, could optimize fuel consumption so that commercial planes could fly more efficiently."

Morphing wings can also be useful for military defense and homeland security when applied to unmanned surveillance planes that need to fly quickly to a distant point, loiter at slow speed for a period of time, and then return, Lesieutre explains. Flying efficiently at high speed requires small, perhaps swept, wings. Flying at slow speed for long periods requires long, narrow wings. The morphing wings designed by the Penn State team can change both wing area and cross-section shape to accommodate both slow and fast flight requirements.

The essential features of the Penn State concept are a small-scale, efficient, compliant cellular truss structure, highly distributed tendon actuation, and a segmented skin. The cellular truss structure is the skeleton of the wing. The skeleton is formed of repeating diamond-shaped units made from straight metal members connected at the angles with bendable or compliant-shape memory alloys. Tendons in each unit, like the ropes that shape a tent, can pull the units into new configurations that will spring back, thanks to the shape memory alloys, when the tendon tension is released.

Since the underlying structure can undergo radical shape change, the overlaying skin of the wing must be able to change with it. Lesieutre says a concept that he thinks holds great promise is a segmented skin composed of overlapping plates, like the scales of a fish. He notes that conveyers on the baggage carousel in airports are composed of a similar pattern of plates.

So far, the design team has built a tabletop model of the compliant cellular truss structure and a computer graphic model of the wing structure. The next step will be to design a full-size wing prototype.

"LOOK MA, NO FUEL": LASER-POWERED AIRCRAFT

Ever since the dawn of powered flight, it has been necessary for all aircraft to carry onboard fuel—in the form of batteries, liquid fuel, solar cells, or even a human "engine"—in order to stay aloft. Now a team of researchers from NASA's Marshall Space Flight Center in Huntsville, Alabama, NASA's Dryden Flight Research Center at Edwards, California, and the University of Alabama— Huntsville is trying to change that.

The team has developed and demonstrated a small-scale aircraft propelled solely by an invisible, ground-based laser. The laser tracks the aircraft in flight, directing its energy beam at specially designed photovoltaic cells carried onboard to power the plane's propeller. "The craft could keep flying as long as the energy source, in this case the laser beam, is uninterrupted," says Robert Burdine, Marshall's laser project manager for the test. "This is the first time that we know of that a plane has been powered only by the energy of laser light. It really is a groundbreaking development for aviation."

"We feel this really was a tremendous success for the project," added David Bushman, project manager for beamed power at Dryden. "We are always trying to develop new technologies that will enable new capabilities in flight, and we think this is a step in the right direction." Without the need for onboard energy, such a plane could carry scientific or communication equipment, for instance, and stay in flight indefinitely. The concept offers potential commercial value to the remote sensing and telecommunications industries, according to Bushman. "A telecommunications company could put transponders on an airplane and fly it over a city. . . . The aircraft could be used for everything from relaying cell phone calls to cable television or Internet connections."

Laser-power beaming is a promising technology for future development of aircraft design and operations. The concept supports NASA's mission-critical goals for the development of revolutionary aerospace technologies. A prime military application for the technology is surveillance. The craft could also be used to provide communications coverage for troops within a specific geographic area, or to broadcast radio and TV programs to civilians located in an enemy-occupied city.

The plane, with its 5-foot wingspan, weighs only 11 ounces and is constructed from balsa wood, carbon fiber tubing, and, like the robotic birds, is covered with Mylar film. Designed and built at Dryden, the aircraft is a one-of-a-kind, radio-controlled model airplane. A special panel of photovoltaic cells, selected and tested by team participants at the University of Alabama—Huntsville, is designed to efficiently convert the energy from the laser wavelength into electricity to power a small electric motor that spins the propeller.

The lightweight, low-speed plane was flown indoors at Marshall to prevent wind and weather from affecting the test flights. After the craft was released from a launching platform inside the building, the laser beam was aimed at the airplane panels, causing the propeller to spin and propel the craft around the building, lap after lap. When the laser beam was turned off, the airplane glided to a landing.

The team made a similar series of demonstration flights in 2002 at Dryden, using a theatrical searchlight as a power source. The recent flights at Marshall are the first known demonstrations of an aircraft flying totally powered by a ground-based laser. The demonstration is a key step on the road toward the time when we can beam power to a plane aloft.

BEETLE-INSPIRED DESIGN: PULSE COMBUSTION

The bombardier beetle, which defends itself by squirting predators (ants, frogs, spiders) with a high-pressure jet of boiling liquid in a rapid-fire action called pulse combustion, may provide the key to significant improvements in aircraft engine design.

The bombardier beetle's unique natural combustion technique is being studied to see if it can be copied for use in the aircraft industry. Scientists at Britain's University of Leeds, who are studying the bombardier beetle's jet-based defense mechanism, hope it will help them solve a problem that occasionally occurs at high altitudes: How to reignite a gas turbine aircraft engine (including many different types of military aircraft), which has cut out when the outside air temperature is as low as −50°C.

Building on work by Professor Tom Eisner at Cornell University, the new project will set out to improve understanding of the beetle's unique pulse combustion and nozzle ejection mechanism. It also aims to identify how combustion engineers could exploit this understanding to practical effect. It could, for example, lead to the development of a device that helps relight aircraft engines at high altitude by more accurately squirting plasma into the engine's combustion chamber.

The project team is led by Andy McIntosh, a professor of thermodynamics and combustion theory at Leeds' Energy and Resources Research Institute. "The bombardier beetle's defense mechanism represents a very effective natural form of combustion," says McIntosh. "Copying such natural mechanisms is part of the growing field of biomimetics where scientists learn much from intricate design features already in nature. Understanding this beetle better could lead to significant advances in combustion research."

The project, which is funded by the UK's Engineering and Physical Sciences Research Council (EPSRC), involves computer-based numerical and mathematical modeling. The initial focus is on understanding the beetle's heart-shaped miniature combustion chamber, which is less than 1 millimeter long. Simulations for a larger chamber, around a few centimeters long, in which gases are ignited by raising the chamber's surface temperature will then be conducted. The effects of different-shaped nozzle outlets and explosion chambers will also be examined.

If the bombardier beetle's combustion technique sounds familiar, you may be recalling the series of repeated explosions (pulse combustion) used to power the Doodlebug V1 flying bomb of World War II. Each low-pressure part of the combustion cycle drew in more fuel, which was exploded in the high-pressure part of the cycle and then ejected.

GOOD VIBRATIONS: VEHICLE DAMAGE DETECTOR

Just as a spider strums specific fibers of its web and listens for returning signals to detect prey, a technique developed at Purdue University uses vibrations to pinpoint damage in composite materials for future military vehicles.

The vibration approach, developed by Douglas E. Adams, an assistant professor of mechanical engineering at Purdue, can automatically diagnose the structural integrity of composite materials; that is, materials made of layers of ceramics, plastics, metal alloys, and fabrics, all held together in a glue-like matrix. Because they are strong, yet lightweight, such composite materials are increasingly being used in missiles, aircraft, and other weapons systems, including a new type of armor in future tanks.

Although this armor will be far more effective than the metal armor employed in today's vehicles, the composite material does have an Achilles' heel: Whereas damage in metal armor is easy to spot, composite materials sometimes appear undamaged on the outside when there is serious damage on the inside, according to Adams.

The new vibration-based technique he has developed could be used to continuously check the integrity of the composite armor, and issue a warning if the material is about to fail. The technique has proved to be sensitive enough to detect damage caused even by small impacts, such as those that might occur in the field—a wrench hitting the side of a tank, for example. "The method could apply equally well to commercial aluminum air-frame fuselage skins or to transportation infrastructure such as bridges and railways for subways and trains," Adams says.

Adams and coresearchers Shankar Sundararaman and Timothy Johnson, both Purdue graduate students, and mechanical engineer Elias Rigas from the Army Research Laboratory, have found that significant damage can be caused inadvertently in the field during transport when heterogeneous structures made of composite materials are dropped or struck with an object. "This impact damage can cause the part to catastrophically fail," Adams says. Damage from impacts or wear can also cause layers of the composite materials to delaminate, essentially separating from each other and weakening the affected area.

The diagnostic system the researchers have developed uses a series of vibrating actuators and sensors placed around the edges of a part. The actuators transmit high-frequency acoustical waves that hit defects in the material and scatter back toward the transmitter, where the sensors pick them up. "Depending on how that scatter is distributed we can tell how big the damage site is, and we can tell where it is, which is precisely what spiders do to locate prey," Adams says. "They send out propagating waves that bounce off the prey. Their tactile sensitivity is extraordinarily fine."

The diagnostic method has been shown to be very sensitive, says Adams. "We haven't been able to hit a structure with anything below a foot-pound of energy and not see the effects. That's what you would get if you dropped a wrench from, say, 3 or 4 feet onto one of these parts."

Other researchers have used similar techniques, but they have embedded a large number of sensors and actuators throughout the composite material, which weakens the material. "What we are doing is using a relatively sparse array of actuators and sensors on the perimeter of a structure," Adams says. "Our sparse arrays do no harm, which is the first requirement for any structural health–monitoring system, and [they] are much easier to maintain than a widely embedded array if a transducer happens to fail."

Purdue researchers are now working on ways to integrate the method into military weapons systems. One possible application will be to detect damage in ramps used to transfer equipment from one ship to another in high seas. Another possible application is in the fan assembly that will enable the Joint Strike Fighter, the upcoming stealth tactical aircraft being designed for use by the U.S. Air Force, Navy, and Marine Corps, to take off and land vertically.

Adams has previously developed a radar-like diagnostic technique in which sensors were placed at specific structural locations, such as the sites of rivets or bolts, that are prone to damage. That method was limited to detecting damage only at those locations. The new technique can detect damage no matter where it is located. "We can cover a much larger area this way," Adams says. The method also can be tuned to look for damage in specific directions and to cancel out interference from other vibration and energy sources, such as engines or rotating parts. In addition, the software algorithm used in the method is adaptive, meaning it can reconfigure itself in the event of a transducer failure to make the best use of the remaining sensors.

THE TIMBOT: ROBOTIC VEHICLE CONTROL

Computer scientists at Oregon Health and Science University (OHSU) have stripped down a radio-controlled monster truck and turned it into a miniature vehicle that's helping them perfect the latest generation of robotic command software.

The Timbot (Fig. 5–1) is equipped with its own computer system, a video camera, and other sensors. On a very basic level, it

FIGURE 5–1.   TIMBOT.

can decide where it needs to go, using its sensors and an onboard computer, and, at the same time, transmit live video images across the Internet so that a remote viewer can see what Timbot is looking at.

The Timbot is one part of DARPA-funded Project Timber in the Pacific Software Research Center. It is called an embedded system because the software is embedded inside another system (in this case, a robotic monster truck) and serves the specific needs of that system (in this case, guiding the vehicle's movement).

"Actually, embedded systems are all around us," says Mark Jones, an associate professor of computer science and engineering at OHSU. "Many devices—from household appliances to medical devices, bank ATMs, automobiles, and aircraft—have computers embedded in them. Nobody likes having to reboot a desktop computer that has crashed, but the consequences of a bug in the software that controls embedded systems like these could be much more serious."

While it may look like a toy, Timbot is actually a sophisticated tool used for testing the original software developed at the university's School of Science and Engineering that may one day guide unmanned robotic vehicles such as cars, buses, or even aircraft. The Timber project is developing new software that will make it easier to construct more reliable embedded systems, and is using Timbot to demonstrate how these technologies might be used in practice. "Think of what happens when you give someone driving directions," says Jones. "I [will] tell you how to drive from downtown Portland to the OHSU West Campus, but I won't need to tell you how to operate your vehicle or to remind you to stop at red lights or purchase gas if you need it. In the same way, Timbot will operate in a largely autonomous manner, responding to high-level instructions about where it should go, but taking care of the details by itself."

Timbot is helping its creators develop systems that support "graceful degradation," adapting flexibly and dynamically to changes in the environment instead of failing outright under system overload. When Timbot encounters challenging conditions, such as an obstacle in its path, that require extra computational power, it will automatically cut back on some of its other functions instead of freezing up or crashing. "For example, if the Timbot needs to perform extensive calculations to ensure that it avoids an obstacle, then it can slow down and reduce the amount of time that it spends processing video. Once it is past the obstacle, Timbot can reallocate its resources, increasing the quality of the video images that it transmits, and moving faster again." In the future, small, remotely controlled ground vehicles such as Timbot could be used by the military to snoop on enemies—silently and under the cover of darkness—to enter places such as buildings, caves, and bunkers that are hidden to aircraft and satellite surveillance technologies. Future versions of Timbot could also be used to lead full-size vehicles across minefields and other types of hazardous terrains.

Timbot is in its early stages of development. While it is capable of some simple navigation by itself, for the most part Jones and his research associates now control it through a wireless link to a laptop computer. But, even at this early stage, the research team is learning about the software challenges of getting Timbot's video, sonar, steering, and locomotion systems to work together.

DRIVING BY BRAIN:
UNDERWATER MANEUVERS

Even the least graceful among us has motor control the most high-tech unmanned undersea vehicle (UUV) would envy, thanks to a region of the brain that allows our bodies to carry out complex maneuvers. The ONR, which traditionally relies on the power of the human mind to achieve breakthroughs in science and technology, is now harnessing the working principle of the brain to control the maneuvers of UUVs.

During the summer of 2004 at the Naval Undersea Warfare Center in Newport, Rhode Island, a mobile autonomous research vehicle (MARV), fitted with an agile "brain-based" controller, smoothly and quietly maneuvered itself in and out of a docking tube. This tricky feat could be critical to future missions in which UUVs might carry out missions too dangerous for humans.

ONR project sponsor Tom McKenna says that the controller, developed jointly by Russia's Nizhny Novgorod State University and Institute for Applied Sciences and New York University Medical School, mimics the part of the human brain that controls balance and limb movement, known as the olivo-cerebellar system. Engineers at Nizhny Novgorod built the integrated circuits that serve as a model of the agile controller. McKenna explains that it represents a "weakly chaotic system" of neurons coupled in a pattern that enables the controller to emulate the function of the olivo-cerebellar system.

The controller can be used to replicate not only the human body's ability to carry out complex maneuvers but also, for example, the wing control of birds and insects as they adjust their angles of flight. In the case of the MARV, the controller will manipulate the movements of high-lift actuators that change the direction and speed of a vehicle's motion. This capability could be exploited both by autonomous military and commercial systems that require highly precise movement control.

SMART DROPS: PINPOINT AIR SUPPLY

With precision airdrop, the air force and army plan to eventually safely deliver anything from sensors to armored vehicles in weights ranging from 200 to 42,000 pounds to friendly ground forces with accuracy similar to Joint Direct Attack Munitions, commonly called smart bombs, that strike enemy targets.

The next step toward making that a reality is the Joint Precision Airdrop System (JPADS), which is intended to resupply troops anytime and anywhere within 24 hours, where 24 hours is worst case from United States to anywhere in the world. Aircraft survivability will increase because cargo will be delivered within 100 meters of the ground target from altitudes of 25,000 feet. The ACTD will focus on payloads of 10,000 pounds—the lightweight category—with a usable payload of no less than 8,000 pounds, which would resupply troops with food, water, ammunition, and even fuel, according to Richard Benney, technical manager for JPADS and Airdrop Technology Team leader at the U.S. Army Soldier Systems Center.

Cost is the driving factor for JPADS. The capability already exists, but at more than 5 times the cost users are willing to pay, according to Benney. The goal is to drop the price to $3 to $6 per cargo pound, but, even at that price, he says, it's an expensive alternative to current, standard low-altitude airdrop systems. "It won't replace the ground logistics, but it gets you the extra capability, especially if you're cut off by an ambush and need resupply, or are in a location that trucks can't reach," says Benney. "It won't drop a Humvee—the next [weight] level will do that, [but] a lot of the technology from this program applies to all weight classes."

Even with advanced technology, Benney notes that "smart" systems won't allow flight crews to drop supplies anywhere and expect a precise landing. Rather, it widens the window of opportunity to make it easier. JPADS combines the army's Precision and Extended Glide Airdrop System (PEGASYS) program with the air force's Precision Airdrop System (PADS) program to meet joint requirements for precision airdrop.

PEGASYS is the name of a family of precision airdrop systems, consisting of extra light, light, medium, and heavy payload categories. It consists of a canopy decelerator and airborne guidance unit, including a GPS, along with the appropriate pallet platform. PADS is an onboard computer system predicting release points for ballistic or "dumb" parachute systems for high-altitude airdrops. It uses mission-planning and weather-forecasting software, and can receive en route mission changes and weather updates via satellite links. The joint system will be able to send a signal from the aircraft to the receiver of cargo pallets carried aboard a C-130 or C-17, and each pallet potentially can be directed to different drop zones.

"The mission-planning software will be able to communicate with any airdrop system," says Benney. "The pilot or navigator, possibly via a SATCOM link from anywhere in the world, will be able to tell each individual load where to go. They could be spread out or bunched together or both depending on what's needed." To get similar accuracy now, cargo needs to be released at 1,500 feet or lower, and, even then, only the first pallet will land close to the intended target because the aircraft generally crosses a 3-mile drop zone to deploy all the payloads it is carrying. That allows enough time and distance to take hits from shoulder-launched missiles or antiaircraft artillery, says Benney.

There are three candidate decelerator systems for JPADS: a low-cost parafoil, a hybrid, single-surface parachute, and a "strong screamer." The parafoil uses low-cost parachute construction techniques similar to round parachute designs, but offers greater capability and reliability. The hybrid is a new design built with a lower-cost, high-performance, zero-porosity fabric used in the hot air balloon industry. The screamer starts with a small speed-reducing parachute deployed at high altitude, which then opens standard army inventory round parachutes at lower altitudes. JPADS expects to ultimately select just one of these decelerators as it prepares to meet the needs of the Objective Force of just-in-time resupply to locations anywhere around the world.

WASTE NOT: CONVERTING HEAT INTO ELECTRICITY

"Waste heat" might not be such a waste after all. The excess heat produced in everything from microelectronics to large ship engines is generally thought of as a problem for engineers to solve. But a new leap in semiconductor technology funded by ONR could put that troublesome heat to good use.

"With this class of semiconductors, when you have a temperature gradient you can generate electrical current," explains Mihal Gross of ONR's physical sciences division. "Or if you pass an electrical current through the material, you can get a temperature gradient for cooling."

An ONR-funded research group at Michigan State University led by Mercouri Kanatzidis has found the right combination of ultra-pure lead, antimony, silver, and tellurium for a material, called LAST, that is significantly more efficient for high-temperature power generation than existing thermoelectric materials.

"The navy is looking at the material's power-generation potential," says Gross. "We have the potential to exploit regions on a ship or land vehicle where there is waste heat, and use it to produce electricity." Because the material can be produced in bulk, its uses could one day include replacing today's shipboard steam plants, which run generators, with solid-state modules of LAST that would produce electricity directly. Although the research is still ongoing, it holds the promises of extending vehicle range, or providing the energy necessary to power a wide range of electrical and electronic devices without the need to carry extra fuel.

THE "OTHER" WAR

So far we've looked at an array of technologies that are designed to help the military fight a conventional war, one that's fought with guns and ammo. But as we've all learned in the days after 9/11, wars can also be fought in the shadows. This "other" type of war, conducted against enemies that try to melt into the fabric of everyday life, requires new and powerful tools designed to gather critical information about anonymous foes and to detect both imminent and long-term threats. The United States doesn't have much experience in this type of warfare. But thanks to an emerging generation of "shadow war" technologies, it's a war the nation and its allies have a much better chance of winning.

CHAPTER SIX

THE SHADOW WAR

SECURITY AND CRYPTOGRAPHY

HIDDEN MESSAGES, LOCKS, chemical sniffers, surveillance cameras—all things not usually thought of as weapons. Yet it's these tools of the "shadow war" that can assist soldiers in the field by protecting military secrets and helping friendly forces surreptitiously look into the enemy's strategies and tactics.

In this new age of terrorism and shadowy opponents, technology can also help governments detect the first signs of a chemical, biological, or radiological attack, providing precious minutes that can be used to help safeguard innocent civilians.

"AGENTS" ON A MISSION

Thousands of special "agents" created at the Department of Energy's ORNL are on missions 24 hours a day as they work to uncover threats to national security. These agents, which are actually intelligent software programs, scan the Internet, satellite images, hundreds of newspapers, and electronic databases worldwide as they search for anything that even hints at a plot. In addition, the agents reproduce and spin off special-purpose agents that assist in the massive effort to scan more data than is humanly possible to analyze.

"The challenge is to take an incredible amount of information and very quickly determine what represents a true threat to our safety," says Thomas Potok, who leads a team of researchers in the lab's computational sciences and engineering division. "It's like having a stack of 100,000 pages and having to find the 20 pages that contain information critical to national security."

By using computers to gather data and reduce the information to what is relevant, the intelligence community can concentrate on analyzing just the meaningful information. Thus, quick and accurate decisions can be made based on hard data instead of on instinct or gut reactions.

"We're trying to marry what people do best with what computers do best so we can reduce the amount of information that we have to deal with," Potok says. ORNL's intelligent software agent research actually began in the late 1980s and has involved a number of clients, including the military, the intelligence community, Battelle (an independent high-tech research and development laboratory that works closely with the federal government), and DOE.

For the military, Potok describes a future battlefield in which intelligent software agents gather information from multiple sources, analyze it instantly, and send information to a commander or command center. As a result, instead of a commander being bombarded with information and having to mentally determine priorities, the officer is fed information in order of its importance.

Turning to the homeland, cameras at airports, seaports, sporting events, and other major, public gathering places can be linked to agents that quickly scan the scene for potential threats. Researchers create agents for this purpose by, for example, programming them to look for objects that are out of place or anything that has changed since the last scan.

"With satellite imaging and the many other tools we have at our disposal, it gets rather sophisticated," says Potok, adding that his colleagues are a creative bunch, who write programs that result in highly effective agents. "In creating intelligent agents, we think beyond the normal bounds of software engineering," Potok says. "We look at biological and natural models such as a school of piranha or a flock of birds as patterns for our agents. We also look at breeding and natural selection as a blueprint for finding solutions to complex problems."

The challenges are immense, but so are the rewards. "Ultimately, our goal is to be able to detect an imminent threat that no one has been able to see with conventional methods," Potok says. Remaining challenges include scalability, which involves figuring out how thousands—or even millions—of sensors and agents can communicate with each other and with people. Another challenge involves developing agents that more closely mimic brain functions. While ORNL has made great progress in the area of intelligent software agents, Potok expects greater progress as ORNL's computing power continues to increase.

QUANTUM CRYPTOGRAPHY: SECURING INFORMATION WITH NOISY LIGHT

Put aside images of World War II espionage and code breaking. Today, cryptography is vital to the security of a form of communication and commerce never imagined 60 years ago: the Internet. Researchers at Northwestern University have demonstrated a new high-speed quantum cryptography method that uses the properties of light to encrypt information into a form of code that can be cracked only by violating the physical laws of nature.

In the open and global communication world of the Internet, information security is a critical issue because conventional cryptographic technologies cannot be relied upon for long-term security. Once optimized, the Northwestern method could replace the mathematical cryptography currently used by businesses, financial institutions, and the military for secure communication. The innovative protocol promises security even against information security's greatest foe: the not-yet-invented but still-feared quantum computer, so powerful it could break almost any conventional code.

"As computing power and data traffic grow and information speeds get faster, cryptography is having a hard time keeping up," says Prem Kumar, professor of electrical and computer engineering at the McCormick School of Engineering and Applied Science and coprincipal investigator on the project. "New cryptographic methods are needed to continue ensuring that the privacy and safety of each person's information is secure."

According to Kumar, "Our research team has succeeded in encrypting real information, sending the message over [the] University fiber-optics system at very high speeds, and decrypting the information, which is no small feat. Other quantum cryptography methods are slow and impractical for long-distance or high-speed communication, whereas ours shows great potential for real-world applications."

The researchers transmitted encrypted data at the rate of 250 megabits per second. Because it uses standard lasers, detectors, and other existing optical technology to transmit large bundles of photons, the Northwestern protocol is more than 1,000 times faster than its main competitor, a technique based on single photons that is difficult and expensive to implement. "No one else is doing encryption at these high speeds," says Kumar.

The Northwestern method, which at present is geared toward securing the public fiber-optic infrastructure, uses a form of "secret key" cryptography. In this type of cryptography, the two people communicating, say Alice and Bob, have the same secret key. If Alice wants to send a secure message to Bob, she sends a message in a "locked box," which Bob can open. To encode her message Alice uses the key to manipulate the light, creating a pattern more complex than just "on" or "off." The method takes advantage of the granularity of light, known as quantum noise, which is integrated with the secret key's pattern. (Random polarization is one way to change the light's granularity.) To someone without the key, let's say the eavesdropper Eve, the information is indecipherable—the stolen message contains too much "noise." Bob, with the secret key, has the pattern and can receive the signal with much less noise, allowing him to read Alice's encoded message.

Having demonstrated that their high-speed encryption protocol works on a real network with real data, the researchers now are working toward speeds of 2.5 gigabits per second, which is the rate at which regular information is currently transmitted over the Internet's fiber-optic network.

"Current cryptographic schemes are vulnerable because as computers get more powerful the cryptography gets slower due to longer and longer keys," says Horace Yuen, professor of electrical and computer engineering with a secondary appointment in physics and astronomy. He is principal investigator and theorist on the cryptography project. "What we offer is a quantum cryptography system that is unconditionally secure, fast, easy to manage, and cost efficient. Our technology promises a realistic security solution to increasing computing power. We expect to develop a practical application within 5 years."

The quantum cryptographic research project is supported by a 5-year, $4.7 million grant from DARPA. In addition, the Northwestern research team is working with two industrial partners, Telcordia Technologies of Red Bank, New Jersey, and BBN Technologies of Cambridge, Massachusetts, to develop prototype systems for integration into the core optical networks of the Internet. Northwestern has filed a number of patents based on the technology developed at the university.

MICROWAVES: BRINGING CONCEALED WEAPONS TO LIGHT

Microwaves could provide a safe new way of finding hidden weapons and buried mines, thanks to research being conducted in the United Kingdom by a team of engineers and physicists at Northumbria University, with funding from the UK Engineering and Physical Sciences Research Council (EPSRC).

Detection systems used in the fight against terrorism and other crimes rely on X-ray radiation to penetrate materials and build up an image of what is underneath. However, because X-rays can damage living tissue, considerable precautions need to be taken when using these systems. Microwave radiation, on the other hand, is harmless to humans and has the potential to produce high-quality, three-dimensional holographic images of objects concealed from view, which may lead to the use of microwaves as a safer alternative to X-rays in airport security checks, building searches, land mine detection, and other applications.

Although technically viable, microwave imaging systems will only be deployed widely if they can produce results quickly and cheaply. To tackle this key barrier, the innovative technique being developed by the new EPSRC-funded project will comprise a two-stage process. The first involves the use of conventional detectors to measure the two-dimensional pattern made by the scattering of microwaves when they come into contact with a hidden object. The second stage takes this data and uses computer software to construct a three-dimensional image. The technique aims to avoid the need to use complex one-stage equipment that produces images slowly and at considerable expense.

David Smith, of the university's School of Engineering and Technology, is leading the project. "The technology could be very versatile and suited to use in security, medical, and industrial applications," he says. "Although we are just at the beginning of this research, our ultimate aim is to offer an alternative, fast 3D microwave imaging technique that can be used across a wide range of disciplines."

SETTING LIMITS: CRACKING DATA HIDING

An electrical engineer at Washington University in St. Louis has devised a theory that sets the limits for the amount of data that can be hidden in a system, and then provides guidelines for how to store data and decode it. The theory also provides guidelines for how an adversary could disrupt the hidden information.

The theory marks a fundamental and broad-reaching advance in information and communication systems that eventually will be implemented in commerce and numerous homeland security applications—from detecting forgery to intercepting and interpreting messages sent between terrorists. Using elements of game, communication, and optimization theories, Jody O'Sullivan, a Washington University professor of electrical engineering, and his former graduate student, Pierre Moulin, now at the University of Illinois, have determined the fundamental limits on the amount of information that can be reliably hidden in a broad class of data or information-hiding problems, whether they are in visual, audio, or print media.

"This is the fundamental theorem of data hiding," O'Sullivan says. "One hundred years from now, if someone's trying to embed information in something else, they'll never be able to hide more than [the amount] determined by our theory. This is a constant. You basically plug in the parameters of the problem you are working and the theory predicts the limits."

Data hiding is an emerging area that encompasses such applications as copyright protection for digital media, watermarking (a means of authenticating intellectual property such as a photographer's picture or a Disney movie by making imperceptible digital notations in the media identifying the owner), fingerprinting, steganography (the embedding of hidden messages in other messages, such as digital pictures), and data embedding.

While data hiding has engaged the minds of the nation's top academics over the past 7 years, it also has caught the fancy of the truly evil. In February 2001, 9 months before September 11, *USA Today* reported that Osama bin Laden and his operatives were using steganography to send messages back and forth.

"The limit to how much data can be hidden in a system is key because it's important to know that you can't hide any more [information] and if you are attacking (that is, trying to disable the message) that you can't block any more than this [amount]," according to O'Sullivan. "It's also important because [if you know] this theory you can derive what the properties of the optimal strategy to hide information [are], [as well as] what the properties of the optimal attack [are]."

While the intellectual pursuit of data hiding is relatively new, with the first international conference on the topic held in 1996, the practice goes back to the ancient Greeks. Herodotus was known to have sent a slave with a message tattooed on his scalp to Mellitus; the slave grew his hair out to hide the message, which encouraged revolt against the Persian king. In World War II, the Germans used microdots as periods at the ends of sentences. Magnified, the microdots carried lots of information. The German usage is a classic instance of steganography.

There will be much work ahead before O'Sullivan's theory will be fully implemented. "This is an example of one kind of work we do at the center that has a big impact in the theory community, but it's a couple of layers away from implementation," O'Sullivan says. "But the theory answers the questions, what is the optimal attack and what is the optimal strategy for information hiding?"

IS IT REAL?: DECODING DIGITAL IMAGES

"Seeing is no longer believing. Actually, what you see is largely irrelevant," says Dartmouth professor Hany Farid. He is referring to the digital images that appear everywhere: in newspapers, on Web sites, in advertising, and in business materials, among others.

Yet, when it comes to military surveillance, it's not only important to know if such images have ever been tampered with, it can be critical. An array of military and civilian intelligence organizations must be able to depend on digital images in order to obtain essential information. Think, for example, of satellite photographs showing an enemy airfield or missile base.

Farid and Dartmouth graduate student Alin Popescu have developed a mathematical technique to tell the difference between a "real" image and one that's been fiddled with. Consider a photo of two competing CEOs talking over a document labeled "confidential—merger," or a photo of Saddam Hussein shaking hands with Osama bin Laden. The Dartmouth algorithm, presented at the Sixth International Workshop on Information Hiding, in Toronto, Canada, can determine if someone has manipulated the photos, for example by blending two photos into one, or adding or taking away objects or people in an image.

"Commercially available software makes it easy to alter digital photos," says Farid, an associate professor of computer science.

"Sometimes this seemingly harmless talent is used to influence public opinion and trust, especially when altered photos are used in news reports."

Photos have been altered in the past—from airbrushing a model's blemishes in fashion magazines to creating images of aliens in tabloid newspapers, and giant lizards in the movies—but computers make it easier for more and more people to manipulate images. Farid explains that "regular" photos are hard to change without special expertise in altering negatives or darkroom privileges that would allow someone to influence the printing process. However, once images have been digitized—translated into the computer language of ones and zeros—it's easier to manipulate them.

A digital image is a collection of pixels or dots, and each pixel contains numbers that correspond to a color or brightness value. When marrying two images to make one convincing composite, you have to alter pixels. They have to be stretched, shaded, twisted, and otherwise changed. The end result is, more often than not, a realistic, believable image. "It's not easy to look at an image these days and decide if it's real or not," says Farid. "We look, however, at the underlying code of the image for clues of tampering."

Farid's algorithm looks for the evidence inevitably left behind after an image has been tinkered with. Statistical clues lurk in all digital images, and the ones that have been tampered with contain altered statistics. "Natural digital photographs aren't random," he says. "[Just as sitting] a monkey in front of a typewriter is unlikely to produce a play by Shakespeare, a random set of pixels thrown on a page is unlikely to yield a natural image. [This] means that there are underlying statistics and regularities in naturally occurring images."

Farid and his students have built a statistical model that captures the mathematical regularities inherent in natural images. Because these statistics fundamentally change when images are altered, the model can be used to detect digital tampering. "This technology to manipulate and change digital media is developing at an incredible rate," Farid adds, "but our ability to contend with its ramifications is still in the Dark Ages. I'm always asked if this technology would stand up in a court of law." The simple answer is, he explains, "eventually." Farid predicts there will be skepticism and a great deal of scientific and legal debate, but, ultimately, he believes that some form of his technology or someone else's will be incorporated into our legal system.

Farid, whose research is funded by an Alfred P. Sloan Fellowship, the National Science Foundation, and the U.S. Department of Justice, also works with law enforcement officials, government representatives, and corporate leaders on this issue of authenticating digital images. "There is little doubt that countermeasures will be developed to foil our detection schemes," says Farid. "Our hope, however, is that as more authentication tools are developed it will become increasingly more difficult to create convincing digital forgeries."

DIAMOND-FILM SENSORS: DETECTING BIOLOGICAL WEAPONS

In this time of the chronic threat of terrorism and the possibility of war with an adversary who may be armed with biological weapons, high on the wish list of security agencies and battlefield commanders is a quick and easy way to detect the presence of dangerous biological agents.

Now, with the help of a novel diamond film developed by chemists at the University of Wisconsin, the age of the inexpensive, compact sensor that can continuously scan airports, subways, and battlefields for the slightest trace of biological weapons may be at hand. Coupled with modern electronics, the new sensors would not only be able to detect nearby biological agents, but also sound alarms and even call for help.

The new technology is centered on a newfound ability to make highly stable, DNA-modified diamond films. The ability to build a stable platform that can constantly sniff for anything unusual—and that can be integrated with microelectronic devices— has long been a problem of surface chemistry. "The real advance is getting the needed chemical stability and then combining that with electronic sensing," says Robert J. Hamers, a professor of chemistry at UW—Madison who collaborates with Lloyd Smith, also a UW—Madison professor of chemistry, to develop the chemistry for the new diamond surfaces, and with Dan van der Weide, a UW—Madison professor of electrical and computer engineering, to achieve the electronic sensing.

"Although there have been many advances in bio-chip technologies, getting a stable platform that can be used for continuous monitoring—not just one-shot analysis—has been a long-standing problem," Hamers says. "And diamond solves it." Biological sensors of the future will need to operate at the interface of biology and modern microelectronics. Not only must these sensors possess the ability to detect biological molecules of interest, they will also need to take advantage of the signal amplification and processing properties of microelectronics. Because diamond films can be deposited on silicon, the stuff of which computer chips and other microelectronic devices are made, it provides a bridge between the world of miniature electronics and biology, which requires a chemically stable platform for biosensing.

Such sensors, according to Hamers, would be about the size of a postage stamp and could be sprinkled in public places such as airports, bus depots, subways, stadiums, and other places where large numbers of people gather. They could act, he says, like a "bio–cell phone, where they just sit in place and sniff, and when they detect something of interest, send a signal" to alert security or sound an alarm. "This is where we are going and we are almost there. The science is there. We've proven we can make surfaces that are much more stable than anything that existed before," he says, "and we've proven that we can detect the electrical response when biomolecules bind to the diamond surface." Hamers acknowledges that before the new biosensors become practical, engineering designs for packaging and fluid-handling systems for sample introduction must be completed. But while some work remains, he says, "the hardest part appears to be over."

In the past, scientists tried in vain to develop surfaces with long-term stability for use as biosensors. But silicon, the material upon which computer-chip technology rests, tended to defy efforts to harness it as a stable surface for sensing biological molecules. "Silicon oxide proved not to be a good material [on which] to do sensing," says Hamers, "[and] in the case of silicon, the best available technology did not permit . . . contact with water for any period of time. It eventually degrades. That was an obstacle to the merging of the microelectronic and biotechnology communities." Other materials such as gold, glass, and glassy carbon proved either unstable or difficult to integrate with silicon.

The biologically modified diamond films, on the other hand, have proven to be remarkably durable, able to withstand multiple cycles of processing DNA genetic material that can diagnose such things as anthrax, ricin, bubonic plague, smallpox, and other molecules that can potentially be used as biological weapons or agents of terror. "You can really abuse it and it doesn't care," Hamers says.

"The diamond films are chemically durable and they are electrochemically durable." In a battlefield environment, such sensors could be deployed on vehicles or scattered across the landscape to warn of the presence of such agents. Early warning could save lives and enable soldiers to prepare to operate in a contaminated environment.

Chips made with diamond films may also have important economic implications in research. One of the most important new technologies in biology is bio-chips or gene chips, a technology that permits scientists to, among other things, scan biological molecules to assess gene activity. Current technology relies on expensive chips that are used once and discarded. "People are putting a lot of time and energy into building bio-chips," says Hamers. "You use them once and throw them away. There can be a lot of money invested in building a single chip. Although probably not useful for clinical applications, if you can reuse a chip in a research environment, it may have important economic implications."

The work of the Hamers and Smith groups on biological modification of diamond has been reported in *Nature Materials,* and at meetings of the Materials Research Society and the American Vacuum Society. The technology's extension to electronic detection was reported in March 2004 at a meeting of the American Chemical Society.

The work was supported by the ONR, the Wisconsin Alumni Research Foundation, the National Institutes of Health, the National Science Foundation, and the Department of Energy.

DETECTION: THREE-TIERED BIO-WARFARE PROTOCOL

The U.S. Navy is now using a new protocol to detect bio-warfare (BW) agents, such as anthrax, aboard its ships. "Until mid-2002, the only equipment to detect biological agents [on] warships . . . were the sailors themselves," says Michael Boehm, an associate professor of plant pathology at Ohio State University and a lieutenant commander in the U.S. Naval Reserve. "The military was ill prepared to deal with what might happen if a 37-cent letter filled with anthrax or smallpox was opened on a ship at sea."

Boehm was called to active duty shortly after September 11, 2001, to help the navy develop an inclusive bio-warfare agent detection program. In late 2001, he headed for the Navy Medical Research Center's Biological Defense Research Directorate (BDRD) in Silver Spring, Maryland. Boehm's active duty stint ended in February 2003, and he returned to Ohio State.

He and his colleagues at BDRD developed, implemented, and trained navy personnel how to sample, test, and respond to possible bio-warfare attacks by agents such as anthrax and smallpox. In spring 2004, the navy adopted this as their standard operating procedure for detecting the presence of BW agents. According to Boehm, the plan can be used anywhere there's a suspected BW incident.

The researchers devised a three-tiered bio-warfare agent detection system:

Level 1: Presumptive. Armed with portable handheld assays, which look and function like home pregnancy test kits, trained personnel can determine within 15 minutes to an hour whether a suspected BW agent has infiltrated a ship. Developed in the early 1990s for use in Operation Desert Storm, such test kits give users quick results, but also have their limits, Boehm says. "While these tests are a good, quick prescreen, the only definitive way to determine if the results of the handheld test are truly accurate is to grow the organisms in a laboratory."

Level 2: Confirmatory. Before the current testing system was in place, shipbound navy personnel had to wait 24 to 96 hours before getting a definitive answer on whether a suspected pathogen had infiltrated a ship, says Boehm. Suspicious samples were sent to land-based laboratories for testing. Under the new protocol, several warships have installed air filters connected to machines that run polymerase chain reaction (PCR) assays—tests that provide a genetic fingerprint of a bio-warfare agent. These air filters "breathe" nearly 70 times the amount of air a sailor breathes. "With PCR, we could find a single gene copy amid an ocean of pathogen in less than an hour," Boehm says. This kind of quick detection helps medical personnel know how to treat people who were exposed to the pathogen, ideally before they have a chance to infect others.

Level 3: Definitive. The suspected specimen is sent to BDRD or another national laboratory, such as the Centers for Disease Control and Prevention or the U.S. Army's Medical Research Institute of Infectious Diseases, for a full analysis. "The problem with BW agents is that they come in a variety of forms, such as bacteria, toxins, and viruses," Boehm says. "Several of the biggest threats—anthrax and plague—are bacteria and can be grown in a laboratory. But viruses like smallpox can only be grown in special conditions. Toxins can't be cultured."

While the three-tiered protocol was designed for seafaring ships, the same steps can be—and have been—taken to determine the presence of BW agents in buildings and other enclosed structures. "BDRD used these three highly complementary approaches for detecting bio-warfare agents to process more than 16,000 environmental samples collected from key points within Washington, D.C., during the anthrax outbreaks following September 11," Boehm says. Since then he and his colleagues have trained personnel from more than thirty naval units to conduct confirmatory analyses.

"SMART DUST" DETECTS BIOTERRORIST AND CHEMICAL AGENTS

University of California—San Diego researchers have developed dust-size chips of silicon that allow them to detect rapidly and remotely a variety of biological and chemical agents, including substances that a terrorist might dissolve in drinking water or spray into the atmosphere. The technique, which uses a laser scanner, could be employed as an advanced warning system for biological and chemical attacks. In addition, it offers the promise of wider commercial use in research and medical laboratories where it can be used to perform rapid biochemical assays, screen chemicals for potential new drugs, and test samples for toxic materials.

For the detection of chemical and biological warfare agents, the advantages of smart dust are numerous. Not only are the smart-dust crystals small, inconspicuous, and capable of detecting thousands of possible agents at once, but they can detect potentially hazardous compounds remotely from a distance. Unlike grocery store scanners, which typically must read bar codes only inches away, Michael J. Sailor, a professor of chemistry and biochemistry at UCSD who headed the research effort, and his group have been able to get their laser to detect the color changes in the smart dust 20 meters away, the length of the hallway outside their research laboratory. With a more powerful laser, he adds, "we're planning to take this outside and see how far we can go. Our goal is 1 kilometer (or about 0.6 of a mile)."

The project, which is supported by DARPA, could be a major asset to homeland security efforts. "The idea is that you can have something [with some intelligence built into it] that's as small as a piece of dust, so that it could be inconspicuously stuck to paint on a wall or to the side of a truck or dispersed into a cloud of gas to detect toxic chemicals or biological materials," says Sailor. "When the dust recognizes what kinds of chemicals or biological agents are present, that information can be read like a series of bar codes by a laser that's similar to a grocery store scanner to tell us if the cloud that's coming toward us is filled with anthrax bacteria or if the tank of drinking water into which we've sprinkled the smart dust is toxic."

The "bar code" on the silicon dust particles basically is a specific wavelength of light, or color, reflected from their surfaces after thin films layered on the silicon chip chemically react to a specific chemical or biological agent. The scientists start with silicon wafers similar to those used in the manufacture of computer chips, then "encode" them, using a special electrochemical etch, by generating layers of nanometer-thick porous films on the wafers. This layered structure on the dust-size particles, which are created by breaking apart the wafer using ultrasound, imparts unusual optical properties to the particles. Referred to as photonic crystals, these micron-size particles are able to reflect light of very precise colors, each of which can be thought of as a single bar of a grocery store bar code. "When you're looking for chemical or biological warfare agents, you're going to want to search for thousands of different chemicals," says Sailor. "Since the particles can be encoded for millions of possible reactions, it's possible to test for the presence of thousands of chemicals at the same time."

The encoding that takes place in these particles provides colors that are so sharp—from the visible to the infrared—a laser can read thousands of distinct colors corresponding to separate chemicals. In this way, the UCSD researchers say these coded particles can perform thousands of biochemical assays in something as small as a beaker or a Petri dish.

In addition, because the smart-dust chips are fabricated from silicon, they can be easily made using existing computer chip technology, and the compatibility of porous silicon with living cells and the long-term stability and nontoxicity of this material makes them especially useful in biomedical applications. "The big advantage of the method is that porous silicon is biocompatible and the use of these encoded silicon nanostructures in medical diagnosis may be significantly better than other methods that involve the use of potentially toxic materials, such as heavy metals," says Frédérique Cunin, a postdoctoral fellow in Sailor's laboratory.

"This is an example of marrying microtechnology, which is used to make microelectronic chips, with silicon chemistry and molecular and cell biology to create hybrid, integrated chip platforms for medical applications," says Sangeeta N. Bhatia, an associate professor of bioengineering at UCSD who also has a medical degree. For example, she says, if a patient has a cough, a blood sample can be sent to the laboratory for screening. DNA probes for various types of infectious diseases could be coded with the crystals, and these probes could be mixed in with the patient's blood sample. If the blood sample binds with one of the probes, its crystal code will exhibit a pattern that identifies the probe, and thus diagnoses the disease that the patient carries. "This technology offers two important advantages," Bhatia adds. "The encoding strategy is quite robust because it is hard wired into the crystals and the crystals are built on a silicon platform, which we know is easily adapted to biological applications."

The smart dust achievement is among a number of new silicon-based technologies developed in Sailor's laboratory in recent years that could be employed to thwart terrorists. Working in collaboration with a team headed by William Trogler, a professor of chemistry and biochemistry at UCSD, Sailor and his group developed an inexpensive and portable nerve gas detector that uses a CD laser to detect the changes of a catalyst on the surface of a tiny silicon chip that reacts to sarin and other nerve agents. The two also developed a method for using tiny silicon wires in a solution to detect trace amounts of TNT and picric acid, a common explosive used by terrorists.

Previously, Sailor's group devised a method of using the explosive properties of silicon in a way that would allow computer chips with valuable security information to self-destruct or allow for the explosive propulsion of tiny information-collecting chips. In addition, working in collaboration with Bhatia's group, Sailor and his team of scientists developed porous silicon chips capable of maintaining fully functioning liver cells, an important advance in the effort to keep liver cells alive outside of the human body.

MINI SPECTROMETER IDENTIFIES BIOHAZARDS

Researchers at the Department of Energy's ORNL have developed a miniature device, the Calorimetric Spectrometer (CalSpec), that can accurately identify biological hazards as little as a fraction of a spore of anthrax (Fig. 6–1) and other biological hazards within 30 milliseconds. It does this by identifying their molecules. The molecular absorption can induce stress changes that allow for an initial detection that can be used for measurement. The identification of chemical or biological molecules, along with DNA/RNA, creates a photothermal signature that allows for detection, identification, and measurement of a substance.

Such prompt detection and identification of hazardous materials could greatly enhance the protection of first-responder emer-

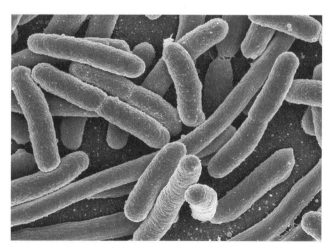

FIGURE 6–1.   ANTHRAX BACTERIA.

gency personnel and the capabilities of early warning systems. Current technologies do not provide the level of sensitivity offered by the CalSpec chemical, biological, and DNA/RNA detection system.

Researchers Panos Datskos and Slobodan Rajiic of ORNL's Engineering Science and Technology Division developed the CalSpec technology. ORNL has licensed the technology exclusively to Innovative American Technology of Herndon, Virginia, and Boca Raton, Florida.

The spectrometer could have a wide variety of applications in commercial industry and in homeland defense, including mass transit and airport security; in the postal industry, to protect workers and the public; and in monitoring air quality systems. "The CalSpec detection device could provide a cost-effective and easily deployed upgrade for these systems to enable rapid detection, greater accuracy, and—most important—increased sensitivity down to a fraction of a spore," says Jack Cummings, vice president of business development for Innovative American Technology.

ORNL and Innovative American Technology are working in collaboration to commercialize the CalSpec technology. The device will be offered as both a laboratory and field-test device for chemical, biological, and DNA/RNA detection.

BIO-DETECTION WITH LIVING CELLS

The ability to analyze and defend against novel biological agents has been strengthened by the development of a new device that can monitor the metabolism of living cells in near real time.

"So far we have been lucky that terrorists have used well-known biological agents like anthrax and sarin gas," says David Cliffel, assistant professor of chemistry at Vanderbilt University, who led the development group working under the auspices of the Vanderbilt Institute for Integrative Biosystems Research and Education. "But how will we respond if one of these groups uses recent advances in genetic engineering to produce an agent that is new and unknown?"

Part of the answer, Cliffel says, is the device he and his colleagues have developed, called a four-channel microphysiometer. It is a modification of a 10-year-old commercial device called the Cytosensor, made by Sunnyvale, California–based Molecular Devices, which measures changes in acidity in a small chamber holding between 100,000 to 1,000,000 individual cells. Cliffel's research team has added three additional sensors so that the machine can simultaneously chart minute-by-minute variations in the concentrations of oxygen, glucose, and lactic acid, in addition to pH.

The added capability is important because the basic metabolism of a cell involves consuming oxygen and glucose and producing lactic and carbonic acid. As a result, monitoring variations in these four chemicals allows researchers to quickly assess the impact that exposure to different chemicals has on the activity and health of relatively small groups of cells.

"I envision having a microphysiometer with an array of chambers," says Cliffel. "One of them contains heart cells, another contains kidney cells, another nerve cells, and so on. Then, when an unknown agent is pumped into all these chambers, we quickly will be able to determine exactly which part of the body it attacks and the response of the affected cells will provide us with important clues about the manner of its attack."

Because of its potential application for bioterrorism and chemical and biological warfare, the development of the device has been funded by the DARPA; however, the microphysiometer potentially has important applications in detecting and assessing the toxicity of environmental pollutants as well as in basic biological research, its developers point out. The microphysiometer consists of a series of reservoirs, switches, rotary pumps, and tiny chambers made from two thin membrane sheets that contain the cell colonies. The original unit also included a single sensor that measured changes in acidity (pH) in the extracellular liquid.

"Over the years, the Cytosensor has been used in a number of studies involving changes in pH," says Cliffel, "but its usefulness was limited because it could only measure a single variable. We realized that analytical chemists had recently developed new techniques that would allow us to simultaneously measure variations in several different key compounds."

Using these techniques, Cliffel's interdisciplinary research team—chemistry postdoctoral assistants Sven Eklund and Dale Taylor working with senior research associate Eugene Kozlov and research professor Ales Prokop from chemical engineering—developed the three additional sensors out of specially coated electrodes. They attached these to another commercial device that has recently come on the market, called a multipotentiostat, which allowed them to take simultaneous readings from the sensors.

One of the biggest problems they had with these modifications was due to the fact that one of the devices was designed to be controlled by a Windows computer and the other by a Macintosh. "In the beginning, there was a tremendous amount of cross-talk between the two computers that we had to eliminate," Eklund says.

The researchers tested the modified device with several different toxic agents and two cell types. In one test they added fluoride to Chinese hamster ovary cells. Fluoride blocks cells' ability to convert glucose into ATP, the chemical that cells use as an energy source. Their measurements showed that the lactate concentration and acidification rate dropped rapidly as the cell slowed its production, while oxygen and glucose concentrations rose as the cell consumption slowed. "We could see the cells basically go into hibernation," says Cliffel. "Then, when we flushed out the fluoride, we could see them start up again."

They ran similar tests with two other known metabolic poisons—antimycin A and 2,4 dinitrophenol—and a type of cell that produces connective tissue called a fibroblast and received similar results. Last year, the Vanderbilt researchers upgraded a Cytosensor at the Edgewood Chemical Biological Center at the Aberdeen Proving Ground in Maryland. Since then their ECBC collaborators have been using the device to study cell response to a number of different chemical and biological agents.

Since submitting the paper in January 2004, Cliffel's group has also successfully tested the device with two pesticides—parathion and paraoxon—and two common pollutants—the gas additive

MTBE and hexachromium, the pollutant that Erin Brochovich made famous. Tests are ongoing, and the researchers are looking to have a model suitable for real-world use available within a couple of years.

READY TO WEAR (TO WAR)

The evolving nature of warfare has even started affecting the clothing warfighters wear. We're not yet at the stage where fighting men and women are about to be routinely clothed in full body armor (a la *Star Wars*), but threats from chemical and biological agents, as well as the ever-pressing need to boost individual performance, is reshaping military "fashion."

Chapter 7 looks at how researchers are now working to create military clothing that's protective, functional, comfortable, better fitting, and, sometimes, even sharp looking.

UNIFORMS, PROTECTIVE GEAR, AND OTHER THINGS THEY DON'T SELL AT BLOOMINGDALE'S

THE WORD *UNIFORM* comes from the Latin words *unus,* meaning one, and *forma,* meaning form. In addition to its original purpose of distinguishing friend from foe, military clothing has long been regarded as a badge of honor and a means of improving the morale and esprit de corps of its wearers.

It was not until the establishment of large standing armies, in the seventeenth and eighteenth centuries, that uniforms were widely adopted. Before this time, armies consisted mostly of retainers and mercenaries. Retainers typically wore their master's livery, while mercenaries put on whatever they liked. The absence of uniforms is largely responsible for the significance attached to the colors and standards, which alone formed rallying points for the soldier and his comrades. In a world without uniforms, a man who left his force's colors wandered into the terrifying unknown, for there was nothing to distinguish friend from foe.

Prior to the advent of uniforms, generals would occasionally order their men to wear some type of improvised badge, such as a sprig of leaves, or the shirt outside of the coat. Such items were, of course, easily lost or hard to discern in the heat of battle. Next, a scarf featuring uniform color was added as a means of identification. By the late eighteenth century, uniforms of the major European powers had evolved into elaborate coordinated wardrobes—particularly for officers.

Long before they were used for identification, military clothing fulfilled a more fundamental role—protection. The most basic protection provided by clothing is, of course, safeguarding its wearer from natural elements, such as rain, cold, and the sun. Since ancient times, items such as armor plate and mail were used to protect soldiers from enemy weapons. Today, researchers are working on an array of novel technologies that are designed to make uniforms more identifiable, protective, and comfortable.

FUTURE WARRIOR: CLOTHES MAKE THE SOLDIER

Future Warrior (FW) is the army's vision of the military uniform of the future. First assembled at the U.S. Army Soldier Systems Center in 1999, Future Warrior was extensively redesigned in 2004 to better reflect technology decades from reality for use in soldiers' uniforms.

While the Objective Force Warrior (OFW) (see Chapter 1) soldier weapon platform should be fielded within the decade, FW is a visionary tool designed for use by researchers, says Cheryl Stewardson, the integrated protection functional area leader for the Natick Soldier Center's OFW program.

Future Warrior was reintroduced at the May 2004 opening of the Institute for Soldier Nanotechnologies, a new partnership between the army and Massachusetts Institute of Technology (MIT). "We wanted to showcase now the concepts they're working on for the future," says Stewardson. "Seeing [concepts] on a human form helps us see how [technologies] might be used and [what] their limitations [might be]." During the past 3 years, scientists and engineers have experimented with concepts that might be used on OFW, Stewardson says, and what was not possible for OFW ended up on Future Warrior.

Replacing the modified motorcycle helmet used in the earlier Future Warrior concept, the custom-designed helmet is leaner and incorporates several features it is anticipated technology currently in development will make possible. For example, a blue-tinted visor signifies agile eye protection against tunable lasers; inside, a new projection display technology, which will be integrated into the Joint Strike Fighter helmet, is more accurately depicted. "We have sensors now for thermal and image intensification, but making them small enough, fusing the images, and projecting them onto the visor—that's the leap," says Stewardson.

Openings at the top of the helmet fit have been designed to accommodate a 3D audio and visual sensor suite. They restore natural hearing lost in an encapsulated space and enhance long-range hearing. Cameras enhance vision from the sides and rear. A smaller halo on the helmet represents a tracking system for friendly and enemy forces. Reshaping the helmet gives Future Warrior an expanded field of vision and hearing.

Protection against chemical and biological agents is more realistic with a respirator tube that attaches to the back of the helmet and connects to a low-profile air purifier that forces cool air into the helmet for comfort and visor defogging. "It was envisioned [as coming] down very sleek into the body, but we couldn't find a material to do it in the short time we had to put this . . . prototype together," Stewardson says.

Another major change in the uniform is the addition of protruding, interconnecting pieces of black plastic to the legs, which represent a lower-body exoskeleton. It will connect through the boots up to the waist and will enable the wearer to carry up to 200 pounds.

Above the waist, MIT's research on nanomuscles—tiny motors that act like living muscle—are designed to generate advanced arm and torso strength, and may be linked to the exoskeleton to give FW potentially superhuman ability to move or carry. A flexible display on the forearm glows when switched on and draws attention to the simulated touch-screen keypad that will be used for information input and output for tasks such as navigation, monitoring physiological status, and command communication. The display is connected to a compact computer worn on an armored belt around the waist.

Attached to the arm is a slim box representing a remote control unit for any system, such as a robotic mule or unmanned aerial vehicle that might be used. Found near the top of the torso front and back are what look like quarter-size buttons built into the fabric. These represent a nanostructure sensor array that may be used to detect weapons of mass destruction, friendly or enemy lasers, or even weather conditions.

"[The sensors] could trigger a response in the uniform to open or close the fibers depending on temperature or precipitation," says Stewardson. The color black was chosen to clue observers that FW is still in the future, she says; in reality, the goal is for a uniform that's invisible. Along the black stretch fabric are custom-fitted plastics and foams that take the place of liquid body armor that will instantly solidify on impact. "All the parts are much harder than we want [them to be]. We haven't figured out how to portray [liquid armor]," says Stewardson.

Indeed, much of the future capability of the uniform can't be shown, at least in part, because nanotechnology (the science of developing materials at the atomic and molecular level) is on the cutting edge of research. Through nanotechnology, multifunctional materials will be able to transport power and data, fend off chemical and biological agent attacks, self-decontaminate, and become waterproof. "I believe nanotechnology is going to give us much more than we can even envision today. This is just a sampling," Stewardson says. FW is still a moving target for researchers, shedding workable technology for the next greatest thing.

"There's always going to be a Future Warrior," Stewardson says. "In the soldier business, you can never rest on your laurels. Somebody is always out there to beat you."

LIFESAVER 1: CUSTOM-FITTED UNIFORMS

The time and cost associated with outfitting military personnel in various types of uniforms and protective garments date back to the earliest days of organized armies. No doubt, in ancient times, more than one Greek foot soldier complained about the way his tunic and breastplate fit.

The problem extends beyond an issue of mere style and comfort, however. In an era when the potential exists for chemical and biological attacks, a poorly fitted garment can be a matter of life and death. Soon, military personnel will be able to step into a booth where a 3D body scanner sends more than 300,000 body data points to a computer. Clothing suppliers can then apply that data to specific clothing styles, fabrics, and design features and produce a custom-fitted garment.

Using software supplied by Lectra, an international company (headquartered in France) involved in the design, manufacture, and distribution of software and hardware for industrial users of textiles, leather, and other soft materials, student researchers at Cornell University are the first in the country to produce automated custom patterns for garments. Using a sophisticated body scanner, which generates an individual's detailed measurements from a 3D image together with the software, which produces patterns encoded for a personal fit, the researchers were able to create accurate, professional-quality patterns for apparel, to grade these patterns to fit a range of sizes, and to experiment with automated custom fit.

"The U.S. population is so physically diverse that the apparel industry can't fit everyone using a standard measurement chart for sizing garments," says Susan Ashdown, associate professor of textiles and apparel at Cornell and an expert on the sizing and fit of apparel. She notes that the technology also has significant commercial potential. "The [apparel] industry is moving toward the mass customization of garments in response to consumer demand. This demand will someday be met, I think, through virtual storefronts with consumers using their body-scan measurements to buy custom-fit clothing on the Internet."

Ashdown is using 3D body-scanning technology in Cornell's teaching labs and as a research tool to provide analyses of fit for specific target markets and to improve the fit of apparel. Using the computer software, Ashdown's students created sizing charts and special alteration grades for different body types, and set up the custom software to generate patterns based on body measurements. Log House Designs, a New Hampshire manufacturer of outerwear, produced custom-fitted jackets for ten individuals scanned by the students for this project. Ashdown reports that the fit of the final set of jackets was very successful.

LIFESAVER 2: STRONGER, LIGHTER BODY ARMOR

Two new fibers are vying to one day replace the respected but heavier Kevlar, the staple of body armor for decades, as the army strives to enhance mobility by reducing the soldier load.

Body armor is one of the more riveting individual equipment success stories to come out of the ongoing conflicts in Afghanistan and Iraq, where there have been reports of dozens of saved lives directly attributed to the bullet-stopping and shrapnel-halting ability of the helmet, flexible vest, and rigid chest plate combination worn by troops. Yet, although it protects well, body armor ranks with water, ammunition, and weapon as the heaviest items worn or carried by troops, according to engineers on the Ballistics Technology Team at the U.S. Army Soldier Systems Center.

"The army is putting the best available armor materials into soldiers' armor," says Philip Cunniff, a research mechanical engineer. "Part of our work in the Ballistics Technology Team is to develop new materials and techniques to lighten the load of those armor systems."

Body armor technology has advanced in the past century to protect the head and torso against high-velocity handgun bullets and fragmenting munitions, such as those from artillery shells, mortar shells, mines, and grenades. Lightweight, small-arms protection is also now available for the torso.

The nylon flak vest for ground troops and steel helmet from the 1960s were replaced by Kevlar vests and helmets during the 1980s in a product called Personnel Armor System, Ground Troops (PASGT). At the users' request, performance increased with the PASGT system but weight remained about the same, according to Cunniff. The next major change came in the 1990s with an improved version of Kevlar that helped lighten the vest by 25 percent and increased ballistic protection.

Today, the team's objective is to reduce the weight again, this time by 25 to 30 percent, without losing performance. Zylon and M5 fibers show potential in meeting or exceeding that goal. Zylon, a commercially available fiber first developed by the air force in the 1980s and now produced in Japan, turned in a solid performance in testing, says Cunniff. A prototype helmet made in 2003 with Zylon was developed as part of the Human Systems Defense Technology Objective for Ballistic Protection for Improved Survivability. The Zylon helmet weighs 1.79 pounds rather than the 3 pounds the PASGT weighs at the same protection levels.

Cunniff says two possible roadblocks with Zylon are environmental degradation and the law requiring certain military products

FIGURE 7–1.   CUTTING M5 ARMOR.

FIGURE 7–2.   M5 ARMOR PLATE.

to be manufactured in the United States with domestic materials. Zylon has been shown to break down with exposure to light, high heat, and humidity, although Cunniff says there may be solutions to these problems.

An alternative material to Zylon is M5 (Figs. 7–1 and 7–2), an ultra-high-performance fiber developed by Magellan Systems International in Bethesda, Maryland. According to Cunniff's mathematical model for estimating impact performance based on the mechanical properties of armor materials, M5 appeared to provide exceptional performance. In addition, Cunniff's model indicated that M5 at the same protection level could weigh at least 35 percent less than currently available fragmentation armor. So far, the ballistic impact test results from a limited, relatively low-strength sample of M5 are glowing. "We shot it, and [the results were] better than we expected," says Cunniff. "We found there was something wrong with the model: We underpredicted the performance of the material. Of everything we looked at, it looks like [M5] will be a really big improvement in reducing the weight of armor."

Another feature of M5 fiber is excellent thermal and flame protection, which means that in addition to helmets, fragmentation vests, and composites for use in conjunction with ceramic materials for small-arms protective plates, M5 fiber could also be used for structural composites for vehicles and aircraft.

"The military market for ballistic material is cyclic," Cunniff says. "The beauty of this fiber is that it should have a lot of other markets when army demand falls. We're hoping it becomes cost-competitive to Kevlar." The plan is to acquire sufficient quantities of M5 fiber to make a prototype helmet, vest, and small-arms protective plate. "Then we can find out how well high-strength M5 performs and . . . what kind of armor we can develop for Objective Force Warrior and the army," Cunniff says.

WHERE DOES IT HURT?: SMART T-SHIRT HAS THE ANSWER

The old military standard-issue T-shirt and dog tags are taking on new meaning and could someday save a life on the battlefield, thanks to a new "smart T-shirt" designed by the Georgia Institute of Technology, under contract with the U.S. Department of Navy. The Sensate Liner for Combat Casualty Care uses optical fibers to detect bullet wounds, and special fibers to monitor health vital signs during combat conditions.

To use this new technology, a combat soldier attaches sensors to the body, pulls the Sensate Liner T-shirt on, and attaches the sensors to the T-shirt. The T-shirt actually functions like a computer, with plastic optical fibers and conducting fibers woven throughout the actual fabric of the shirt. The truly unique aspect of this design is that there are no seams or breaks in the plastic optical fiber, which circumnavigates the T-shirt from top to bottom.

"The idea is to send a signal from one end of the plastic optical fiber to a receiver at the other end," says Sundaresan Jayaraman, a professor in Georgia Tech's School of Textile and Fiber Engineering and the project's principal investigator. "If the light from one end does not reach the other end, we know the Sensate Liner has been penetrated (i.e., the soldier has been shot)." A signal bounces back to the first receiver from the point of penetration, helping the medical personnel pinpoint the exact location of the soldier's wound.

The receiver is a Personal Status Monitor (PSM)—the twenty-first-century version of a dog tag—and is worn at hip-level by the soldier. In a combat situation, the plastic optical fiber senses the penetration of a bullet and sends the information of the break in the plastic optical fiber to the PSM. The soldier's vital signs—heart rate, temperature, blood pressure, and so on—are monitored in two ways: through the sensors woven into the T-shirt; and through the sensors on the soldier's body; both of which are connected to the PSM. Information about the wound and the soldier's condition is immediately transmitted electronically from the PSM to a medical triage unit somewhere near the battlefield. The triage unit then dispatches the appropriate medical personnel to the scene. "The Sensate Liner can help a physician determine the extent of a soldier's injuries based on the strength of the heartbeat and respiratory rate," says Jayaraman. "This information is vital for assessing who needs assistance first during emergency situations in which there are numerous casualties."

Besides military applications, the Sensate Liner has potential for use by law enforcement personnel. Astronaut suits, athletic outfits, and even children's sleepwear could take advantage of the Sensate Liner's vital signs monitoring component. The Sensate Liner, which is still in the development phase, is expected to cost between $25 and $35.

REQUEST—"SEND WARM CLOTHING": RESPONSE—PROTECTIVE COMBAT UNIFORM

Calling from a bomb crater in Afghanistan in the winter of 2002, the Special Forces Soldier had a pointed request for the Special Operations Forces (SOF) Special Projects Team at the U.S. Army Soldier Systems Center in Natick, Massachusetts: Send warm clothing. About 1 year later, special operators working in frigid battle zones got what they wanted in the Protective Combat Uniform (PCU), an interchangeable fifteen-piece, seven-level ensemble that can be worn in layers appropriate for the mission.

"He said, 'We're cold. You gotta do something to help,' " says Richard Elder, an equipment specialist on the Special Projects Team and project officer for the PCU, recounting the conversation that started the process. "It's exciting that in less than 12 months, the system was fielded into theater. That's never been done before."

The PCU will replace the existing Lightweight Environmental Protection (LEP) developed under the Special Operations Forces Equipment Advanced Requirements (SPEAR), a program to produce modular equipment systems that focus on mission tailoring, enhanced survivability, and enhanced mobility while reducing weight, bulk, and heat stress. The LEP consists of lightweight and midweight underwear, medium-stretch bib overalls, pile jacket, and wind-resistant jacket along with the outer water-resistant shell of the Extended Cold Weather Clothing System parka and trousers. Special operators' only other option was to purchase commercial items on their own.

The PCU takes cold-weather gear to its highest level. "The goal is to give the special operators a system as good or better than anything commercially available and build a system that stays with the commercial market instead of falling behind so you're not getting 6-year-old technology," Elder says. Instead of gathering and assessing clothing sold in stores, the Special Projects Team started from scratch. The team consulted with extreme alpinists and outdoor apparel companies, and followed recommendations from a joint panel of special operators in order to introduce a product the Special Operations community would approve. "We wanted to make sure we didn't overlook anything. As a system, we wanted it completed nationally," Elder says. "This acquisition model has proven itself to be extremely efficient. To build something in real time to meet users' needs is how it should be done all the time."

Wearing the PCU is a matter of mixing and matching the gray garments according to the anticipated conditions and activities of the user. Comfort levels range from −50 to 45 F, and, although there are seven levels of protection, Elder says the clothing in each level is not progressively added or removed the colder or warmer the environment. "We actually get more out of fewer pieces by training the SOF operator how to pack and because of the efficiency of the clothing itself," he says.

Elder says the key to staying warm is moisture management. The latest Polartec fabrics by Malden Mills insulate and wick moisture away from the skin, while outer garments made with silicone-encapsulated fibers by Nextec Applications allow sweat to escape at the same time as it is highly water- and wind-resistant. The idea is to remove moisture faster than the wearer can produce it. The product also breaks new ground for military protective clothing with antimicrobial fibers, a stretch shell, and a design that functions as a complete system through its seaming, grading, and fabrics.

Army Rangers, Marine Force Reconnaissance, Army Special Forces, and Navy SEALs successfully evaluated the uniforms in Alaska in August 2002. By the time the uniform officially fields in 2006, the product will have been upgraded several times with another shell system and alternate vest as part of a catalog of components to further adjust to the specific mission. Until full fielding, those who need the uniforms are getting them and their comments from the battlefield are aiding in the evolution of the design.

"They like it. They're taking it as soon as they can get it," Elder says. "It was exactly what they were looking for. They're even wearing it outside of the profile it was designed for. It speaks well to the system that they're even doing that."

Level 1: A durable, silk-weight Polartec Power Dry fabric worn next to the skin wicks away moisture and dries fast. It consists of a crewneck T-shirt and boxer shorts.

Level 2: A long-sleeve shirt and pants made from Polartec Power Dry fabric worn next to the skin for extra warmth in extreme conditions; wicks away moisture quickly from skin and dries fast. An inserted side panel of Polartec X-Static fabric enhances fit and flexibility. The top has a front 15-inch zip for extra venting and a soft lining around the collar. Comfort features include an articulated side seam on the pants to minimize chafe on the kneecap.

Level 3: A mid-layer jacket made from Polartec Thermal Pro fabric that is water repellent and yet able to breathe. It is worn as an outer jacket in mild temperatures or as a heavy insulative layer in extreme cold. Seamless shoulders, which are then lined for extra warmth, and padding for heavy pack straps minimize chafe.

Level 4: The soft wind shirt is made from an encapsulated microfiber that repels water but also breathes; designed for a variety of conditions. It can pair with a next-to-skin layer for intense activity in cooler temperatures or with the Level 5 soft shell as a mid-layer. It stuffs into its own pocket for easy packing.

Level 5: The key to the entire system, this soft shell fabric jacket and pants are made with fibers encapsulated with silicone that are highly stretchable, windproof, water repellant, and breathable. They are paired with Level 1 or 2 next-to-skin layers, ready for any cold-weather aerobic activity.

Level 6: A lightweight, waterproof, and coated-nylon hard shell slightly oversized to fit easily and quickly over gear. The jacket features water-resistant zippers and armpit zips for maximum ventilation, pocket openings to quickly access inside layers, and a hood that incorporates a stiff brim. The pants borrow the same design from Level 5 but provide waterproof protection.

Level 7: For extreme conditions, this lightweight, loft-insulated level in a jacket, vest, and pants has the feel of down but retains its warmth when wet. Silicone-encapsulated fabric sheds water and is paired with Primaloft insulation for maximum warmth while the liner pulls away moisture.

STEAM HEAT: WARMER FINGERS

Although the Iraq War was fought primarily under desert conditions, conflicts can also take place in colder climates. In recent history, the Balkans War found combatants fighting the weather as well as human opponents and, as we've just seen, the special ops in Afghanistan have been facing severe cold, too.

A cold environment can have a damaging effect on soldiers. As the body attempts to conserve energy, it shuts off heat to the hands, fingers, and toes, dropping the temperature to these extremities by 40 F, making them susceptible to frostbite. A researcher at the University of Missouri—Columbia is developing a new glove containing flexible heat pipes that will solve this dangerous problem.

"This new glove will be lighter, thinner, warmer, and more comfortable than anything on the market today," says Hongbin Ma, assistant professor of mechanical and aerospace engineering, who started on the project in 2003 and recently completed a prototype of the glove. "We simply use the body heat from the upper arm to warm the fingers."

Each glove, which will be made of polyester, contains five small heat pipes, one for each finger, that are about 14 inches long and 1 millimeter × 2 millimeters in the cross section. Each pipe consists of three sections: an evaporating section, which is attached to the upper arm area; an adiabatic section, which is placed between the finger area and the arm area; and the condensing section, which is attached to the finger area.

According to Ma, the heat is transferred to fluid in the glove through direct contact between the heat pipes and the individual's arm. The fluid, in turn, is vaporized and the vapors bring heat to the fingers. The vapor is then condensed (again becoming fluid), and flows back to the arm section through a wick structure embedded in the heat pipe. In this way, Ma says, the heat will continuously be transported from the arm to the finger.

"The heat transport is dependent on the temperature difference," Ma says. "When the temperature difference between the arm and fingers is higher, like it is during the winter, the heat transport capability will increase. When the temperature difference is low, such as when someone comes in from outside, the glove will automatically adjust the heat transfer capability."

Ma, who also is developing the same device for shoes, is the founder of MU's Research Consortium for Innovative Thermal Management, which develops novel, low-cost cooling technologies and delivers the research results directly to the industry. The consortium is the first of its kind in the United States to focus on heat pipes and phase-changing cooling devices.

TRIGGER-TESTED MODULAR GLOVES

Trigger fingers, as well as the rest of the hand, will be ready to react wrapped under the Modular Glove System developed by the SOF Special Projects Team.

The glove system brings a significant change for the SOF community in hand protection. "It's new and has never been done before," says project officer Stephanie Castellani. "It's a great improvement because they've never had anything baseline that all the [SOF branches] have agreed to, and [the system] lays the groundwork for future improvements with new materials and technology."

More important, the gloves pass the trigger test. "Function is first. They have to be able to manipulate their weapon systems," says Richard Elder. "Safety used to be the primary concern, but if he can't shoot, he'll toss it for something else." Now special operators won't have to buy gloves on the commercial market to find a product that works.

In testing, special operators from different services wore the modular gloves while mountaineering, skiing, and snowshoeing on a glacier in Alaska. Eight companies submitted a glove system through the army's Small Business Innovative Research program, and the glove system developed by Outdoor Research in Seattle, Washington, was chosen in the final selection.

The glove system is composed of a Nomex contact liner, intermediate wet/dry glove, and extreme wet/dry glove with a removable insulation liner. Comfort ranges from −20 to 45 F, depending on which individual glove or combination is worn. In all, there are five ways to dress with the glove system.

The Nomex contact liner was designed for the first layer. It is constructed of a Malden Mills Powerstretch fleece with Nomex and soft, flame-resistant Pittards leather lining the palm and fingers that provide a lightweight, flexible glove with an acceptable grip and abrasion resistance. "This is good alone at temperatures above 40 degrees or when handling hot weapons," Castellani says. "For dexterity and tactility, everyone loved it."

The intermediate wet/dry glove worn with or without the Nomex contact liner protects from 10 to 45 F. Except for the palm, the glove's shell is made with three types of Gore-Tex laminate materials for waterproofing and windproofing while providing moisture vapor transfer and abrasion resistance. AlpenGrip, a proprietary polymer material with a slightly rubbery feel, is used for the palm and provides complete waterproofing and high abrasion resistance while retaining flexibility. Attached inside the glove is a waterproof liner coated with brushed polyester to improve moisture wicking. Even when the intermediate glove is worn over the contact liner, Castellani says tactility is still acceptable. Part of the credit goes to the shape of the glove with its curved fingers and tapered fingertips.

In colder climates, the extreme wet/dry glove protects from −20 to 20 F worn in combination with the Nomex contact liner or intermediate glove. The same AlpenGrip palm with Cordura Gore-Tex material for the shell, waterproof liner with brushed polyester coating, and curved, box-cut fingers with an articulated thumb for dexterity are found in the extreme glove. What's different is the lengthened top portion of the shell, which protects the wrists, and a removable Moonlite Pile insulating insert. Pocket heaters can be placed into either the intermediate or extreme glove, according to Castellani, but the extreme glove insert has a pocket on top designed specifically for that purpose.

The extreme glove also uses hook and loop fasteners at the wrist and forearm for a snug fit. "It's a bit bulkier, but you need the extra bulk for the extra warmth," she says. "It's been tested to −29 F, so it exceeds the −20 requirement."

WEARABLE AIR-CONDITIONERS

Personal protective suits may protect soldiers from chemical and biological weapons, yet extreme heat inside that gear poses a different but equal threat. Without portable cooling technology to ward off heat exhaustion and heat stroke, suits meant to save lives can incapacitate soldiers in just minutes.

Researchers at the Department of Energy's Pacific Northwest National Laboratory are in the process of developing and demonstrating heat-actuated lightweight and compact cooling technology capable of sustaining manageable temperatures inside the protective garb for several hours at a time.

The principles of microtechnology and the very high rates of heat and mass transfer at this miniature scale—about the thickness of the human hair—promise to enable the development of "man portable" cooling systems, weighing in at about 3 to 4 pounds. The system can chill water as it flows through a soldier's vest and is capable of providing relief for up to 6 hours. Instead of using electricity to power a mechanical compressor, heat from burning liquid fuel is used to power the cooling system, thereby replacing bulky, heavy batteries with much lighter fuels. The key for making this portable is microtechnology, which can reduce the size and weight of any existing system by 5 to 10 times.

"This same heat-actuated cooling technology will soon be

used to benefit both military and commercial applications," says Ward TeGrotenhuis, a chemical engineer at the laboratory. "From troops operating in desert environments to astronauts or hazmat teams working in extreme conditions, the same principles apply."

THE "PERFECT MIRROR": TUNABLE FIBERS

MIT researchers have created high-performance mirrors in the shape of hairlike flexible fibers that could be woven into cloth or incorporated in paper. This so-called "perfect mirror" can reflect light from all angles and polarizations, just like metallic mirrors, but unlike its metal counterpart it can also be "tuned" to reflect certain wavelength ranges while transmitting others. As a result, an array of mirror fibers or even a single fiber can be tuned to reflect light at different wavelengths to create a kind of optical bar code that could be woven into fabric or incorporated into a paper to, for example, identify the wearer or for authentication purposes, both potentially useful in the battle suits of future soldiers. Fibers could also be designed to reflect thermal radiation over various ranges, and the resulting lightweight cloth could then be cut into a protective suit. These mirrors could also be used as filters for telecommunications applications.

The work builds on the omnidirectional dielectric reflector (dubbed the "perfect mirror") created in 1998 by Yoel Fink (now an assistant professor in the department of materials science and engineering); Edwin Thomas, the Morris Cohen Professor of Materials Science and Engineering; and John D. Joannopoulos, the Francis Wright Davis Professor of Physics.

The perfect mirror combines the best characteristics of the familiar metallic mirror we gaze into with those of the dielectric mirror, a type of mirror composed of alternating layers of nonmetallic materials that allow much greater control over the mirror's reflectivity, but can only reflect light from a limited set of angles and are polarization sensitive. Dielectric mirrors are most commonly used in high-performance applications such as, for example, in laser cavities or for adding and dropping channels in telecommunications systems.

"We've opened a new avenue of applications for these high-performance optical devices," says Shandon D. Hart, a graduate student who participated in the project. Polymer fibers alone have been quite successful commercially with ubiquitous applications stemming from their superior mechanical properties and low cost. Yet although they've been optimized for everything from strength to moisture resistance (think of a name-brand raincoat), little has been done to control their optical properties, says Fink, leader of the current research team. To address that challenge, the Fink team created a polymer fiber that is essentially sheathed with twenty-one layers of alternating indices of refraction, thus forming a cylindrical perfect mirror.

"Just as in the movie *Honey, I Shrunk the Kids,* wouldn't it be wonderful if you could fabricate something on the macroscale, then shrink it to a microscopic size?" asks Fink. "That's what we did. But the magic shrink-down apparatus we used is not a shrinking beam from science fiction . . . it's a furnace."

The team first created a macroscopic cylinder, or preform, some 20 to 30 centimeters long by 25 millimeters in diameter. It contained the same twenty-one layers of dielectric materials surrounding a polymer core as the final fibers, but unlike the microscopic features of the ultimate fibers, each layer of the preform could be seen with the naked eye. The preform was subsequently fed into a tube furnace that is part of an optical-fiber draw tower recently constructed in the Fink lab.

Fink notes that drawing fibers is a process commonly used to create the glass threads of fiber optics, but while the typical glass thread has only a few fairly large internal features, the mirror threads have over twenty-one microscopic layers. Each layer is only a few hundred nanometers thick, thus spanning nine orders of dimensional magnitude in a single processing step. "The amazing thing is that the resulting fiber retained the same structure as the macroscopic preform cylinder over extended distances," says Fink. "So we're taking the process a step further and getting very high control over the microstructure of the fiber with a very small number of defects overall." Key to the success of the drawing process is the identification of a pair of materials that have substantially different indices of refraction yet similar thermomechanical properties, which enable them to be thermally processed at the same temperature.

The work is funded in part by DARPA through the U.S. Army Research Office and by the Air Force Office of Scientific Research.

"SUNGLASSES": PROTECTION FROM BLINDING LASERS

An enemy laser beam can reach and blind a pilot or soldier in about a billionth of a second. University of Central Florida (UCF) researchers are trying to develop an eyeglass-like device that would react quickly enough to prevent such beams from blinding soldiers, pilots, or police officers, potentially saving their lives.

Working with chemistry researchers at the Georgia Institute of Technology, UCF scientists already have the technology to make objects darken quickly enough to prevent blindness from a laser beam, says Eric Van Stryland, dean of UCF's College of Optics and Photonics. The next step is to incorporate that technology into an object small enough to be worn comfortably by soldiers and pilots.

The UCF-led team of chemists, engineers, and optical scientists wants to come up with a way to fit the technology in a device not much bigger than a standard pair of eyeglasses, says Van Stryland, who is also director of the Center for Research and Education in Optics and Lasers and the Florida Photonics Center of Excellence at UCF.

The new technology works like sunglasses that gradually get darker when the people wearing them step into sunlight and lighter when they return inside. The technology for soldiers and pilots must work a lot faster, as a typical laser beam lasts only about 10 billionths of a second (10 nanoseconds) and travels 1 foot every billionth of a second. At that speed, the damaging laser pulse can reach a pilot flying at 10,000 feet in 10 millionths of a second.

The transparent materials in the device would have to recognize laser beams of any color and, as the atoms and molecules responded to the light, immediately darken to protect the eyes. Basically, the laser beam would provide the energy needed to spark the electronic interactions in the chemicals that would temporarily darken the devices.

Researchers are trying to find a liquid material with atoms that would break up easily to block the lasers and then come back together quickly so that vision is restored. Unlike a solid, a liquid material could break up and come back together several times in response to multiple threats.

While lasers have yet to cause major problems for the military during war, Van Stryland says they could become a threat as laser technology becomes more available and less expensive. Since lasers also could become a weapon of criminals, police officers also could benefit from the device developed by the UCF and Georgia Tech researchers.

The Army Research Office has provided $1 million for the project, and researchers hope to receive more money from the agency in the next few years.

RUMINATIONS AND RAMIFICATIONS

We have reviewed dozens of different technologies, all designed to create a military that's faster and mightier—yet with a smaller fighting force—than the world has ever known.

The United States is often criticized for how it creates weapons systems. Basically, the DoD and a select group of other government agencies create a wish list, award grants, and the researchers go to work. Other countries do it differently. Some countries, such as Germany and Japan, engage in a formal process that brings together government, industry, and academia to evaluate the importance and status of a broad set of technologies. Yet, despite this more systematic planning, they have contributed relatively little to military technology in recent years while promising new technologies are literally flooding the U.S. military. It seems counterintuitive, but it's hard to argue with success, and so it seems highly unlikely that the process is going to change anytime soon.

As we've seen, new technologies promise to give military leaders unprecedented amounts of raw combat power. Yet, as new systems flow into the nation's arsenal at an ever-accelerating pace, some fear that the military is becoming too gadget oriented and wonder if the nation is sacrificing conventional, and often less expensive, military systems in favor of the latest flashy technology.

The answer to this question is a resounding "maybe." It's true that some technologies that looked great on the drawing board turned out to be abysmal failures. Consider the V-22 Osprey. The Osprey's advantages are obvious. This innovative, tilt-rotor aircraft can fly at a maximum altitude of 26,000 feet—about 15,000 feet higher than a helicopter. It can also fly nearly twice as fast and 3 times farther than a helicopter and needs less runway length than a traditional plane—just under 500 feet. Yet the Osprey program has suffered serious setbacks throughout its development, dating back to its first flight on March 19, 1989, and testing is still underway.

But for every high-tech flop, an array of gadgets have not only lived up to their promise, but exceeded them. After all, every technology now used by the military was once somebody's great idea. But that's the thing with research—great ideas sometimes don't pan out. That's why it's called research.

So, where are we headed and when is all this going to end? As technologies become increasingly sophisticated and expensive, is there a logical conclusion to military technology research? And what will the end look like? Will we see drug-energized supersoldiers wielding planet-shattering weapons over a devastated landscape? (That's the Hollywood scenario.) Will warfare be turned over entirely to machines? (That's another Hollywood scenario.) Is research destined to slow down or cease as innovations peter out, or will escalating costs and moral opposition eventually halt research? And, ultimately, will technology truly give America the vital edge necessary to defeat committed and often fanatical adversaries who tend to fight with crude tactics and low-tech weapons?

These are all important questions worth pondering. Yet these are also questions that are impossible to answer—at least, for now. That's because we're far down the technology road, but not far enough to see its end. We can only imagine what our destination will look like. In the meantime, the researchers keep researching, the military keeps buying, and we look on, awestruck, as the parade passes by.

[G L O S S A R Y]

802.11x: A series of IEEE standards for wireless LANs, including 80211.a, 80211.b and numerous others.

agents: Intelligent software programs that search the Internet or a database.

algorithm: A step-by-step mathematical procedure for solving a problem.

anechoic: Free from echoes and reverberations.

asset tracking: Technology used to follow the physical movements of objects and people.

bandgap: The energy difference in a material between its non-conductive state and its conductive state.

bit: The smallest element of computer information.

bits per second: A data network speed measurement. A 10M bps network, for example, has a top data transfer speed of 10 million bits per second.

bluetooth: An open standard for the short-range transmission of digital voice and data between mobile devices.

bps: *See* bits per second.

broadband: High-speed Internet access; faster than 56K bps dial-up service.

buckyball: A spherical carbon molecule, also known as a "fullerine," comprised of sixty atoms. Lighter than plastic and stronger than steel.

cathode ray tube: A vacuum tube that serves as a computer display.

constellation: An array of satellites designed to provide continuous, or near-continuous, access from any point on earth.

CRT: *See* cathode ray tube.

cryptography: The scrambling of plain text into ciphertext (a process called encryption), then back again (known as decryption).

cybersecurity: The protection of computers and networks.

DARPA: *See* Defense Advanced Research Projects Agency.

data hiding: *See* steganography.

Defense Advanced Research Projects Agency: The central research and development organization for the United States.

dense wavelength division multiplexing: A higher-capacity form of wavelength division multiplexing.

Department of Defense: The U.S. Government department responsible for safeguarding the nation's security.

Department of Energy: The U.S. Government department that aims to help the nation achieve efficiency in energy use, diversity in energy sources, a more productive and competitive economy, improved environmental quality, and a secure national defense.

Department of Homeland Security: The U.S. Government department that provides the unifying core for the vast national network of organizations and institutions involved in efforts to secure the nation from terrorists and other threats.

DHS: *See* Department of Homeland Security.

dielectric: An insulator, such as glass or plastic.

digital radio: A radio based on digital technology.

DoD: *See* Department of Defense.

DoE: *See* Department of Energy.

downlink: A communications channel that sends audio and/or video from a satellite to earth.

downstream: A communications channel that sends data from a satellite to earth.

DWDM: *See* dense wavelength division multiplexing.

encryption: The process of transforming plain information into a secure format designed to protect its confidentiality.

ESA: *See* European Space Agency.

European Space Agency: The organization that manages the European space program on behalf of fifteen member states.

FEL: *See* free electron laser.

fiber: *See* optical fiber.

flat panel: A thin display that uses LCD, plasma, or other type of non-CRT technology.

fractal: An object that's self-similar at all scales, in which the final level of detail is never reached and never can be reached by increasing the scale at which observations are made.

free electron laser: A potential weapon that works by generating very large amounts of laser power.

fuel cell: A device that converts a gas or liquid fuel into electricity to power a notebook computer, mobile phone, or other electronic product.

Future Warrior: The U.S. Army's next-generation uniform system.

Galileo: A satellite-based radio navigation system currently under construction by the European Space Administration (ESA).

GHz: *See* gigahertz.

GIF: *See* Graphics Interchange Format.

gigahertz: One billion cycles per second. *See* hertz.

global positioning system: A satellite-based radio navigation system that allows users to find their precise location anywhere on earth.

global system for mobile communications: A second-generation (2G) digital mobile-phone technology based on TDMA, which is the predominant system in Europe and is gaining increasing popularity in North America.

GPS: *See* global positioning system.

graphical user interface: A program that allows users to interact with a computer system in a highly visual manner.

Graphics Interchange Format: A popular graphics file format.

GSM: *See* global system for mobile communications.

GUI: *See* graphical user interface.

haptic interface: Communicating with a computer via touch sensation.

hertz: The basic unit of electrical cycles.

hotspot: A place, such as a home or store, where a wireless connection is available.

human engineering: The science of designing devices and systems to meet the physical and mental needs of people.

IEEE: *See* Institute of Electrical and Electronics Engineers.

IP telephony: The two-way transmission of audio over a network that uses Internet protocols.

IM: *See* instant messaging.

information hiding: *See* data hiding.

instant messaging: The process of exchanging real-time voice or text messages over a network.

Institute of Electrical and Electronics Engineers: A membership organization that sets many telecommunications, networking, and computer standards.

interference: Unwanted signals from a man-made or natural source.

International Organization for Standardization: An international standards-setting organization.

Internet Protocol: The network layer protocol in the TCP/IP communications protocol suite.

IP: *See* Internet Protocol.

ISO: *See* International Organization for Standardization.

Joint Photographic Experts Group: The organization that developed JPEG, a popular image file compression format.

JPEG: A popular image file compression format. *See* Joint Photographic Experts Group.

key: In security, a numeric code used to encrypt information.

kHZ: *See* kilohertz.

kilohertz: One thousand cycles per second. *See* hertz.

LAN: *See* local area network.

laser: A device that creates a uniform and coherent light that can be focused down to a tiny spot as small as a single wavelength.

local area network: A computer network that serves users in a confined location, such as an office or building.

location-based service: A service that works by pinpointing its user's location.

logistics: The procurement, maintenance, and transportation of military matériel, facilities, and personnel.

megahertz: One million cycles per second. *See* hertz.

MEMS: *See* Micro-Electrical Mechanical Systems.

mesh network: A network that provides at least two pathways between each node.

MHz: *See* megahertz.

Micro-Electrical Mechanical Systems: Nano-size devices that are built onto chips.

micro-oscillator: A miniature device for generating tunable microwave signals.

microwave: High-frequency radio signals.

Motion Pictures Experts Group: The organization that developed MPEG, a popular video compression format.

motion tracking: Using a video system to automatically follow a moving person or object.

MP3: A popular audio compression format.

MPEG: A popular video compression format. *See* Motion Pictures Experts Group.

MSO: *See* multiple system operator.

multiple system operator: A cable TV company or other organization that has franchises in various locations.

nanosecond: One-billionth of a second.

nanotechnology: The creation of materials and devices at atomic and molecular levels.

nanotube: A carbon molecule, resembling a chicken wire cylinder, that's approximately a millimeter long and about 1 to 2 nanometers in diameter. Featuring a tensile strength 10 times greater than steel at about one-quarter the weight, nanotubes are considered the strongest known material for their weight.

NASA: *See* National Aeronautics and Space Administration.

National Aeronautics and Space Administration: The U.S. Government agency that operates that nation's space program.

National Institute of Standards and Technology: A U.S. Government agency that develops and promotes measurements, standards, and technologies to enhance productivity, facilitate trade, and improve the quality of life.

National Science and Technology Council: The cabinet-level council that is the principal means for the U.S. president to coordinate science, space, and technology and to organize the diverse parts of the federal research and development enterprise.

National Science Foundation: An independent U.S. Government agency responsible for promoting science and engineering.

National Security Agency: The U.S. Government agency that coordinates, directs, and performs highly specialized activities to protect U.S. information systems and produce foreign intelligence information.

NIST: *See* National Institute of Standards and Technology.

node: In a network, a computer, printer, hub, router, or other connection or interconnection point.

Nomex: Dupont trademark for a temperature-resistant, flame-retardant nylon.

NSA: *See* National Security Agency.

NSF: *See* National Science Foundation.

NSTC: *See* National Science and Technology Council.

Objective Force Warrior: The army's plan to develop a high-tech soldier with 20 times the capability of today's warrior and to have that soldier commissioned by about 2010.

OFW: *See* Objective Force Warrior.

OLED: *See* organic light emitting diode.

olivo-cerebellar system: The part of the human brain that controls balance and limb movement.

omnidirectional: Describes a device, such as a microphone or antenna, that emits or receives signals from all directions.

optical fiber: A thin glass strand designed to carry voice or data signals.

organic light emitting diode: A technology that provides ultra-thin, bright, and colorful displays without the need for space-hogging and power-consuming backlighting.

PAN: *See* personal area network.

passband: A spectrum segment allowed to pass between two limiting frequencies.

personal area network: A short-range network, usually wireless, that provides a connection between two or more devices. Linking a PDA to a computer in order to synchronize data, for example.

photon: A particle of light.

photonic circuit: A circuit that uses light rather than electricity.

photonic crystal: A credit-card-thick stack of optical filters.

piezoelectric: Material that moves when placed under an electric voltage.

plasma: A collection of charged particles containing about equal numbers of positive ions and electrons and exhibiting some properties of a gas.

polymer: A substance made of repeating chemical units or molecules. The term is often used in place of plastic or rubber.

protocol: Rules pertaining to the transmission and reception of information.

quantum cryptography: Technology for encrypting data that draws on inherent properties of photons.

radar: A synchronized radio transmitter and receiver system that emits radio waves and processes their reflections for displaying and locating objects (such as aircraft).

radio frequency identification: An asset-tracking and data-collection technology that uses electronic tags to store identification data and a remote reader to capture information.

reader: A device that obtains data from a source, optically, electrically, or via radio or infrared signals.

RFID: *See* radio frequency identification.

robot: A device that automatically performs complicated and/or repetitive tasks.

SDR: *See* software-defined radio.

sensor: A device that detects a real-world condition, such as heat, motion, or light and converts and relays that information to a computer.

smart: Intelligence built into a device or system.

software-defined radio: A radio that can be instantly adapted to accommodate any standard, simply by loading in various programs.

Speech Application Language Tags: A document language format code that makes speech applications accessible from GUI-based devices, such as PCs and PDAs.

speech integration: Technology that adds voice services to enterprise phone systems and Web sites.

speech recognition: *See* voice recognition.

stealth: An aircraft or other vehicle designed to be invisible, or nearly invisible, to radar and other detection techniques.

steganography: An encryption technique for hiding a message inside an image, audio, or video file.

surveillance: The observation of an area or of people or objects.

tag: An RFID device that contains information about a particular asset. Also a document language format code.

TCP/IP: *See* transmission control protocol/internet protocol.

TDMA: *See* time division multiple access.

teleconference: An audio or audio/video conference of geographically dispersed people using a telecommunications network.

telematics: *See* vehicular telematics.

telemedicine: Healthcare practiced over distance by a network connection.

testbed: An environment used to test a specific project.

thin film: A coating layer so thin that only its surface properties are used.

third-generation services: High-speed multimedia digital mobile phone services.

time division multiple access: A second-generation (2G) mobile-phone technology that interleaves multiple digital signals onto a single high-speed channel.

transmission control protocol/internet protocol: A communications protocol developed under contract from the Department of Defense to internetwork dissimilar systems.

UAV: *See* unmanned aerial vehicle.

ultra wideband radio: A radio that uses ultra-short pulses to distribute power over a wide portion of the radio frequency spectrum. Because power density is dispersed widely, UWB transmissions ideally won't interfere with the signals on narrowband frequencies.

unmanned aerial vehicle: An aircraft that is self-controlled or remotely controlled, by a human or machine, from the ground, a ship, or another aircraft.

uplink: A communications channel that sends audio and/or video from earth to a satellite.

upstream: A communications channel that sends data from earth to a satellite.

UWB: *See* ultra wideband radio.

VCSEL: *See* vertical cavity surface emitting laser.

vehicular telematics: Vehicle-based information, entertainment, and navigation systems.

vertical cavity surface emitting laser: A specialized laser diode designed to improve the speed and efficiency of fiber-optic communications.

VoIP: *See* voice over internet protocol.

voice over internet protocol: A form of IP telephony that allows people to place telephone calls over Internet connections.

Voice recognition: The conversion of spoken words into computer-usable data.

WAN: *See* wide area network.

waveguide: A device for confining and directing electromagnetic waves.

wavelength division multiplexing: A technology that utilizes multiple lasers to send several wavelengths of light simultaneously over a single optical fiber. Each signal travels within a separate color band.

WDWM: *See* wavelength division multiplexing.

wearable computer: A computer that can be attached to its user's body or worn as a garment.

webconference: A text, audio or text/audio/video conference of geographically dispersed people using the Internet's World Wide Web.

Web services: Software that knows how to talk to other types of software over a network. A Web service can be nearly any type of application that has the ability to define to other applications what it does and how it can perform that action for authorized applications or parties.

wide area network: A computer network that serves users in multiple locations, may be regional, nationwide, or even global in scope.

Wi-Fi: A certification for 802.11 wireless network products that comply with Wi-Fi alliance specifications. Also used as a slang term for 802.11 wireless network products in general.

wireless local area network: A local area network that uses a radio technology, such as 80211.x, to interconnect nodes.

wireline: Telephone service provided by wire or cable, as opposed to mobile phone service.

WLAN: *See* wireless local area network.

WPAN: *See* personal area network.

INDEX

[ABOUT THE AUTHOR]

John Edwards is a veteran business-technology journalist who covers emerging trends for a wide range of publications and organizations, including *The Economist,* PricewaterhouseCoopers, *CIO* magazine, *CFO* magazine, IEEE Computer Society, *Oracle* magazine, and *Wireless Week.* His work has also appeared in the *New York Times,* the *Washington Post,* the *Philadelphia Inquirer, Men's Health,* and *American Way,* the in-flight magazine of American Airlines.

The author of *Leveraging Web Services: Planning, Building, and Integration for Maximum Impact,* which explores the next-generation Internet services, John Edwards is currently working on a book about emerging telecommunications technologies.

Mr. Edwards is a dual U.S.-UK citizen, and lives near Phoenix, Arizona, with his wife and two highly independent cats. To learn more about John Edwards, and view some of his recently published magazine articles, visit his Web site at www.john-edwards.com.